Simply SILK

12 Creative
Designs for
Quilting and
Sewing

Mary Jo Hiney

kp **krause publications**
An Imprint of F+W Publications

700 East State Street • Iola, WI 54990-0001
715-445-2214 • 888-457-2873
www.krausebooks.com

Our toll-free number to place an order or obtain
a free catalog is (800) 258-0929.

Library of Congress Control Number: 2007924847

ISBN 13: 978-0-89689-548-5
ISBN 10: 0-89689-548-3

Designed by Rachael L. Knier
Edited by Tracy L. Conradt

Printed in USA

Acknowledgments

Simply Silk is a compilation of sewn projects, many of a quilted nature, some with a focus on journaling as art. They are meant to fill you with inspiration and confidence, urging you to create with silk and dispelling any preconceived notions or fears. Silk is a mysterious fabric to many, perceived to be difficult to work, expensive to purchase, and lacking ease of care. On occasion this is true. At the same time, silk is famously known for its luxurious nature, vibrancy of color, and unique naturalness. The word "silk" conjures up an air of exclusivity, but I want you to know that silk is for you and for your projects.

Working with silk feels good. Its natural fibers are genuine and palpable. *When it comes to color and sheen, none can compare, as silk fibers dye beautifully, producing colors rarely seen with other fabrics.* I hope the pages of this book will inspire you to explore, expand and create with silk. You will be pleasantly surprised with its cooperative nature and thoroughly convinced to forever include silk as a medium of choice. Throughout the pages of *Simply Silk*, you will find tidbits of wisdom, inscribed food for thought to enjoy while in the midst of many creative endeavors.

I would like to take this opportunity to thank Tracy Conradt, Jay Staten and Rachael Knier at Krause Publications for their patience, encouragement and guidance. I thank Candy Wiza at Krause Publications for the appreciation of my vision and her excitement for a book filled with silk projects. Thank you to Bernina of America for their graciousness in allowing my use of the Bernina Artista 730 for all the projects in *Simply Silk*. I want to thank my family and friends for never ceasing to enjoy my newly finished offerings. I thank my kids for expanding my view of the world and always telling me how beautiful my work is. And I thank my husband for believing in me when I have not believed in myself.

Dedication

For Lauren Price. How lucky I have been to work with you again. Your passion for beautiful design and workmanship is a treasure that I will recall often when I am unable to ask you in person, "What would you do, Lauren?"

Table of Contents

CHAPTER 1

Taming the Mysterious and Delicate Silk

TAKE A LITTLE TIME TO CATCH UP on the history of silk, after which you can learn a few tricks and some sewing silk basics that will transform silk into the fabric of cooperation.

HISTORY LESSON AND FOR YOUR INFORMATION

According to legend, in 2640 BC (or BCE), the Chinese princess Xi Ling Shi was the first to reel silk from a cocoon that had dropped into her cup of tea. The process of farming, harvesting and weaving silk became a closely guarded secret for the next 3000 years, known only to the Chinese. From China, woven silk was exported throughout the whole of Asia via the Silk Roads and by sea to Japan. Two monks sent on a mission by Emperor Justinian in 552 AD (or CE) smuggled silkworm eggs to Byzantium. They had hidden the silkworm eggs inside their bamboo walking sticks! From there, the sericulture, or rearing of silkworms for the production of raw silk, spread into Asia Minor and Greece. Currently, India is the second largest producer of silk after China and the largest consumer of silk in the world.

Silk comes from several commercial species of silk worms and the process begins when the silk moth lays eggs. The larvae voraciously feed on mulberry leaves, generally, before entering into the cocoon stage. The protective cocoon is spun by a protein based, jelly-like substance from glands at the top of its head. The worm forms around itself by secreting fibroin protein along with a gum called sericin. The silk hardens when it comes into contact with air. It takes five to eight days for a silkworm to complete its cocoon. Before the silkworm can metamorphose into a moth, the harvesting process begins.

The first stage of harvesting is known as sericulture. Farmers collect the cocoons and deliver them to a factory where the cocoons enter into a filature operation. In this step, the cocoons are sorted according to color, size, shape and texture, then put through a series of hot and cold immersions to soften the sericin (the outside gummy substance). In the filature, or reeling process, silk filaments are obtained from the cocoon, each of which can reach a length of up to 1600 yards, which is why silk is the strongest of natural fibers. The filament is unwound from the cocoon, then joined and twisted with filaments from three to 10 other cocoons to produce a thread of raw silk. These skeins are packed into bundles, called books, which are exported to the mill, where the silk fiber is woven into yardage by hand or machine. It takes about 5500 silk worms to produce one kilogram of silk.

The shimmering appearance of silk comes from the fibers' triangular prism-like structure which allows silk cloth to refract incoming light at different angles.

SILK TERMS

Momme refers to the weight of the silk fibers. A 6 momme (mm) is scarf weight, whereas a 22 mm is suit weight.

Sericin is the gum that protects silk fiber in its natural state. It is not always removed before being spun into a yarn.

Spun silk refers to short silk threads that are spun together to form a longer filament, often used for washable silks.

DESCRIPTION OF SILKS USED FOR PROJECTS

Brocade Heavyweight satin with a Jacquard design, usually blended with rayon.

Chiffon burnout A blend in which the ground fabric is of one fiber and the pile of another. A chemical is applied to the fabric in a brocade-like pattern. When the chemical comes in contact with the pile, the pile is burned away, leaving the ground fabric unharmed.

Crepe de chine Durable, wrinkle resistant, lightweight silk with great drapability. It is a plain-weave fabric made from twisted fibers producing a matte and pebbled texture.

Dupioni Also spelled *douppioni* or *dupion*. Can refer to shantung. Woven from two silk worms that make their cocoons at the same time, nestled together. The entangled cocoon filaments create a slubby weave when woven.

Habutai Often referred to as *China silk*. Soft and lustrous, with a smooth surface and delicate drape. The word *habutai* means soft and downy in Japanese. It is available in different momme weights and is most often used in scarves or for lining.

Jacquard An intricate weaving system creating a complex design, found in many types of fabric, often creating a tone on tone pattern design.

Linen-weave with slubs Heavyweight fabric with a distinctive irregular finish.

Metallic Crinkle Silk fiber woven with metal, then mushroom pleated to form a crushed appearance.

Noil Spun silk with a nubby texture and elegant patina. Has a natural, casual feel.

Organza Plain weave silk of a sheer nature made of highly twisted fine yarns.

Shantung Similar to Dupioni, but of a finer weave and texture, it is named for the Chinese province where it originated.

GETTING STARTED

THE FABRIC OF COOPERATION

One simple step changes the entire process of sewing with silk, turning it utterly into the fabric of cooperation and that step is the application of fusible interfacing. My absolute favorite interfacing to use is a lightweight, fusible knit. This interfacing, a knit tricot fabric, is soft and delicate. It does not alter the hand of the silk, but it changes the structure of the silk so that sewing it is as easy as working with cotton. Imagine that! Quarter-inch seams are a piece of cake.

Sometimes, I will fuse the knit interfacing to the silk before I cut out the required pieces. I generally fuse first when most of the piece of silk will be utilized for a project, and I actually prefer this method. It does use more interfacing, but is tremendously time saving. Other times, I will fuse the silk after cutting out the required pieces. Choose the method you would personally prefer, based on the circumstances.

Another favorite interfacing I use is lightweight, fusible cotton. Fusible cotton will add a lot more body to the silk than the fusible knit. I generally use cotton interfacing for projects requiring more body, such as for a handbag.

The pliable nature of both the knit and cotton interfacings is an essential ingredient for success in sewing silk, in my opinion. I feel nonwoven interfacings are not suited to working with silk.

Keep in mind that the projects in *Simply Silk* are mostly of a quilted nature. In that regard, my suggestions for working with silk pertain to projects of this type. Working with silk for sewing a garment could require somewhat different strategies.

SEWING SILK BASICS

Care of silk Silk fibers are a protein, similar to the fiber content of hair, and of themselves do not shrink. Shrinkage in yardage or as a garment occurs in silk as a result of the fabric's weave type when individual fibers are twisted together with differing consistency. During the laundering process, water releases a twisting energy in the fiber, similarly to what happens to a rubber band when twisted. This is the cause of shrinkage. It is safer for a product label to suggest dry cleaning for this reason.

But, most silk is washable if it has been preshrunk prior to becoming a finished product. Determine ahead of time whether the project you intend to make will need to be dry cleaned or laundered, either by machine or hand. Perhaps you envision never having to wash the project you create. I generally plan on dry cleaning the items I've sewn from silk, and thus, do not preshrink fabrics before working on a project. Certain types of silk, such as those with a shiny satin finish, may be stained with water. Test scraps of silk for your project with soapy water to be certain of the outcome when you desire to be able to launder your project. The hand of some silks will change dramatically, becoming even more supple, once laundered.

These guidelines are merely suggestions, pertaining to a project you intend to make from this book. It is impossible to determine how a ready-to-wear product will react in regard to care.

Needles Consider the type and weight of the silk in your project and the kind of sewing that will occur, whether general or decorative. Universal and Microtex® Sharps are used for general sewing with basic threads. Machine embroidery, Metafil™ and Metallica® needles are used for machine embroidery with specialty threads, as the eyes are larger and the front grooves are deeper on these needles. Needle sizes for all projects in this book should range from size 70(10) to 90(14).

Threads For general construction, all purpose threads are suitable, such as cotton-wrapped polyester core or long-staple polyester. For an amazing treat, use silk machine sewing thread. For machine embroidery, use cotton, rayon, polyester, silk or metallic threads.

GENERAL INSTRUCTIONS AND TECHNIQUES

APPLIQUÉ METHODS

There are several appliqué methods that vary in appearance and approach. You should choose the appliqué method that appeals most to you. I personally prefer finish-edge appliqué.

Raw-edge appliqué No seam allowance is necessary. Fusible web is applied to back side of fabric. Cutout appliqué piece is fused in place. Raw edges are machine sewn or hand embroidered in place, using a stitch of choice. For this method, appliqué pieces can also be pinned in place or lightly glued in place, rather than using the fusible web, then quilted. Regardless of style, edges must be at least marginally sewn in place.

Needle-turn appliqué A ⅛" – ¼" seam allowance is necessary. Appliqué pieces are pinned and then hand-sewn in place with one thread layer, turning raw edges under while stitching. Many like this method, finding it a relaxing form of handwork.

Finish-edge appliqué A ¼"- seam allowance is necessary. Paper, cardboard or freezer paper patterns are used for this method. Appliqué pieces are cut out with seam allowance. Raw edges are pressed upward onto paper or cardboard. Inward edges and points must be clipped to seam line. Paper is removed, then appliqué piece is pressed again. The prepared piece is either hand-sewn or machine sewn in place. This is my preferred appliqué technique.

For machine appliqué, try using the serpentine or blind-hem stitch to machine sew pieces in place, rather than the oft-times-used buttonhole stitch. Both stitches have a more modern and less invasive appearance, blending into a composition rather than hogging the focus. In fact, with size adjustments, many utilitarian stitches can be decoratively used for machine appliqué.

BEADING TECHNIQUES

Sewing single beads in place Bring the needle to surface. Slip needle through bead. Sew back into surface close to entry point. For durability, sew single beads in place two times. Stitch thread invisibly to next bead spot, if in close proximity. Take two tiny stitches to slightly secure thread at new location. Bring needle again to the surface and continue.

Sewing a sequin in place with a seed bead Bring needle to the surface. Slip needle through sequin and then through seed bead. Sew around seed bead and back through sequin, into fabric at entry point. Secure thread on underside and invisibly stitch to next sequin spot, if in close proximity.

Making a bead dangle Fold a length of thread in half, matching ends (if possible, use four thread layers). Thread ends through needle eye. Sew into fabric at beginning position for dangling beads and sew needle through thread loop. Pull thread tight at surface, creating a knotless entry. Sew needle through multiple beads of desired amount for length of bead dangle, having the last bead be a seed bead. Stitch around the last bead and then back up and through all previous beads. Sew thread into original entry point several times, then sew thread to next position for dangle. If working with four thread layers is not possible, sew a second time through all beads when durability is a concern.

EDGE PRESSING TECHNIQUE

This is a fantastic technique for pressing when it is nearly impossible to press a seam allowance open. Fold over the upper layer of the seam allowance and press it flat, in essence pressing it half open, exposing the seam line. Turn item right side out.

FREE-MOTION QUILTING TECHNIQUE

Free-motion quilting is accomplished by inserting the darning foot and lowering the feed dogs on your machine. Lowering the feed dogs allows you to move the fabric being sewn 360 degrees in one movement. You can create an overall meandering stitch or detailed patterned stitch with this method. If you have never tried it before, just pretend you are driving on your fabric. The fabric is the road and the darning foot is your car. At first, you might make jerky stitches, but you will become comfortable over time and generally, once your composition is complete, no one will be able to point out where you turned a corner too sharply. Some newer machines have stitch regulators, which are special foot attachments. A stitch regulator gives much greater control to stitch length and is very desirable for this reason.

MACHINE GATHERING STITCH

Stitch length is at least 4mm. Sew two rows of stitches directly next to each other without crossing over either row, as that will lock the thread. To gather, gently pull either top or bottom thread.

CHAPTER 2

The Sweet Life

JOURNALING HAS BECOME an important aspect of documenting our lives, and the approach for journaling as art differs. Fabric is just another medium in which to journal and silk is wonderfully cooperative is this regard. To incorporate a written message into fabric as art, the Sweet Life offers you a spring board.

You will enjoy the full-sized alphabet as appliqués for creating ABC Expressions. Portable Pages provides an opportunity to quietly express your inner thoughts in lovely compositions graced with a wide variety of embellishments. Heart Etchings provides a pretty place for daily written journaling, swatching or sketching, and Creature Comforts will pamper you.

Just another little note to consider: Be kinder than necessary. Everyone you meet has a story untold.

ABC Expressions

EXPRESS YOURSELF. Through appliqué, love letters are worked onto silken stripes to create this chair-back shrug. The appliqué can be accomplished by using your favorite method and the striped ruffle is made from unsewn, torn strips. Create just one for a special chair, create an entire set, or modify the design for a pillow. Choose to appliqué words that lift the spirit.

MATERIALS

Silk fabrics:
  One each 2¾" x 44" torn strip of 9 different silk dupioni or shantung: terra cotta, cool pink, willow, fawn, rosy brown, pumpkin, new fern, persimmon, rich rose

  ⅝ yd. 44" raspberry dupioni

  5½" x 6½" piece of azalea dupioni

Other supplies and tools:
  1 yd. 20"– 22" lightweight knit fusible interfacing

6" x 17" piece tear-away or cut-away machine embroidery stabilizer

¼ yd. paper-backed fusible web (optional)

2 sheets 8½" x 11" quilter's freezer paper (optional)

19" x 25" piece silk, wool or cotton batting

Sewing machine with basic machine embroidery ability plus basic accessories

Sewing threads: neutral or matching

Machine embroidery thread-accent

Fray preventative

Iron and ironing board

Self-healing cutting mat

Rotary cutter

Grid-lined ruler

Silver marking pencil

Patterns: Alphabet

Finished size: 17¼" x 23½"

CUTTING GUIDE

Torn strips:

Cut each strip in half (2¾" x 22") for shrug. Group one set of half strips (1 of each shade) and set aside. Cut the remaining strips into four 5" cuts for ruffles. Group ruffle cuts into two sets of 18 pieces each, with two of each shade in a set.

Raspberry dupioni:

Cut one piece 18¼" x 21" for shrug backing. Cut four 12" x 2" pieces for ties. Cut two 19" x 2" pieces for ruffle binding. Cut one 11" x 6" piece for L, O and E lettering.

Sheer knit fusible interfacing:

Cut ten 2¾" x 22" strips. Cut one 11" x 6" piece for L, O and E lettering. Cut one 5½" x 6½" piece for V lettering.

STABILIZE THE SILKS

1 Apply fusible knit interfacing strips to wrong sides of 22" silk strips, piecing interfacing by overlapping as necessary when fusing. Apply fusible knit interfacing to wrong sides of 11" x 6" raspberry silk piece and 5½" x 6½" azalea silk piece.

SEW AND QUILT THE SHRUG BODY

Use a scant ⅜" seam allowance unless otherwise noted.

2 Sew 2¾" x 22" strips together, right sides facing, forming the vertically striped piece. Press seam allowances open.

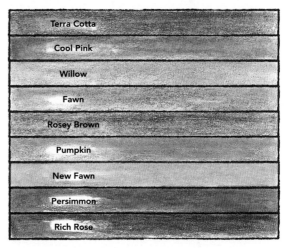

Step 2: With right sides facing, sew the 22"-long strips together in the illustrated color sequence.

3 Layer the vertically striped piece on top of batting. Pin-baste layers together.

4 Crease piece in half to find center. Machine-quilt horizontally across vertical stripes, beginning at center crease. Space horizontal rows 2" apart. Stay stitch along bottom edges. Trim piece 18¼" x 21".

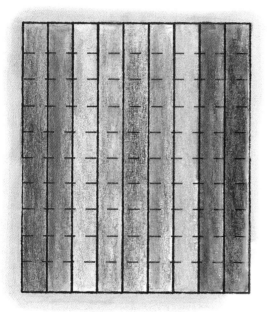

Step 4: Beginning at the center, machine-quilt horizontally across the vertical stripes.

MAKE THE TIES

5 Press raw edges of ties lengthwise to center and then pressed folded edges lengthwise together. Machine sew outer pressed edges together. Trim tie ends at an angle and coat with fray preventative.

6 Pin and baste stitch ties to shrug side edges just above bottom-edge seam allowances.

Step 6: Baste ties to side edges.

BACK THE SHRUG

7 Pin backing to striped piece, right sides facing. Sew the long edges. Press seam allowances open and turn right side out. Press flat.

PREPARE AND APPLIQUÉ
THE LETTERING

8 Apply machine embroidery stabilizer to wrong sides of raspberry and azalea silk lettering pieces. Trace lettering onto right side of fabric, using silver pencil. Machine embroider lettering with assorted sized dots, using machine embroidery accent thread. Remove stabilizer. Press.

9 Choose your favorite method to appliqué the lettering:

Raw-edge appliqué: No seam allowance necessary. Fusible web is applied to back side of fabric. Cutout lettering is fused in place. Lettering edges are machine sewn or hand embroidered in place, using a stitch of choice.

Needle-turn appliqué: ⅛" – ¼" seam allowance necessary. Lettering is pinned and then hand-sewn in place, turning raw edges under while stitching.

Finish-edge appliqué: ¼" seam allowance necessary. Freezer paper patterns, which you must cut out, are ironed onto fabric wrong side. Lettering is cut out with seam allowance. Raw edges are pressed upward onto freezer paper. Inward edges and points must be clipped to seamline. Pull off freezer paper, then press appliqué piece again. Either hand sew or machine sew prepared piece in place. As an option, the paper patterns included in this book can be utilized in the same manner as freezer paper patterns, but without the sticky aspect of the freezer paper.

10 Prepare and appliqué lettering to lower half of striped piece, using method of choice. Hand-or-machine sew lettering in place. For machine appliqué, use a piece of scrap fabric to sample stitches on scrap fabric, including utilitarian styles. When pleased with stitch choice, appliqué letters in place.

MAKE THE RUFFLE

11 Working with one set of 5" cuts for the ruffle, fold one piece in half, wrong sides facing. Machine gather-stitch placing stitches ⅜" up from raw edges. Overlap a second folded piece about ¼" onto the first and continue stitching. Carry on adding folded lengths and gather-stitching in this same manner. Sew a second row of gathering stitches ⅛" from first row. Repeat with second set of cuts for the second ruffle.

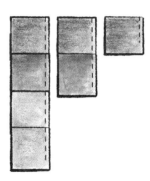

Step 11: Chain gather-stitch by machine the folded ruffle pieces.

12 Pull thread ends to gather ruffle. Adjust gathers so that ruffled edge fits bottom edge of striped piece. Pin and sew in place through all layers. Repeat for the top edge.

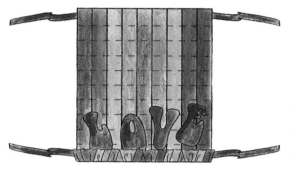

Step 12: Sew ruffle to bottom edge.

FINISH THE RUFFLE EDGE

13 Press binding strip in half, matching long edges.

14 Pin raw edges of binding to bottom edge of striped piece on side with ruffle and sew with a ⅜" seam allowance. Stitch again ⅛" from first row of stitching. Trim seam allowances to a scant ¼". Fold binding around to backing side. Fold binding ends inward and pin pressed binding edge over ruffle seamline. Hand sew pressed edge in place.

Variations in chair shrug colorations and wording.

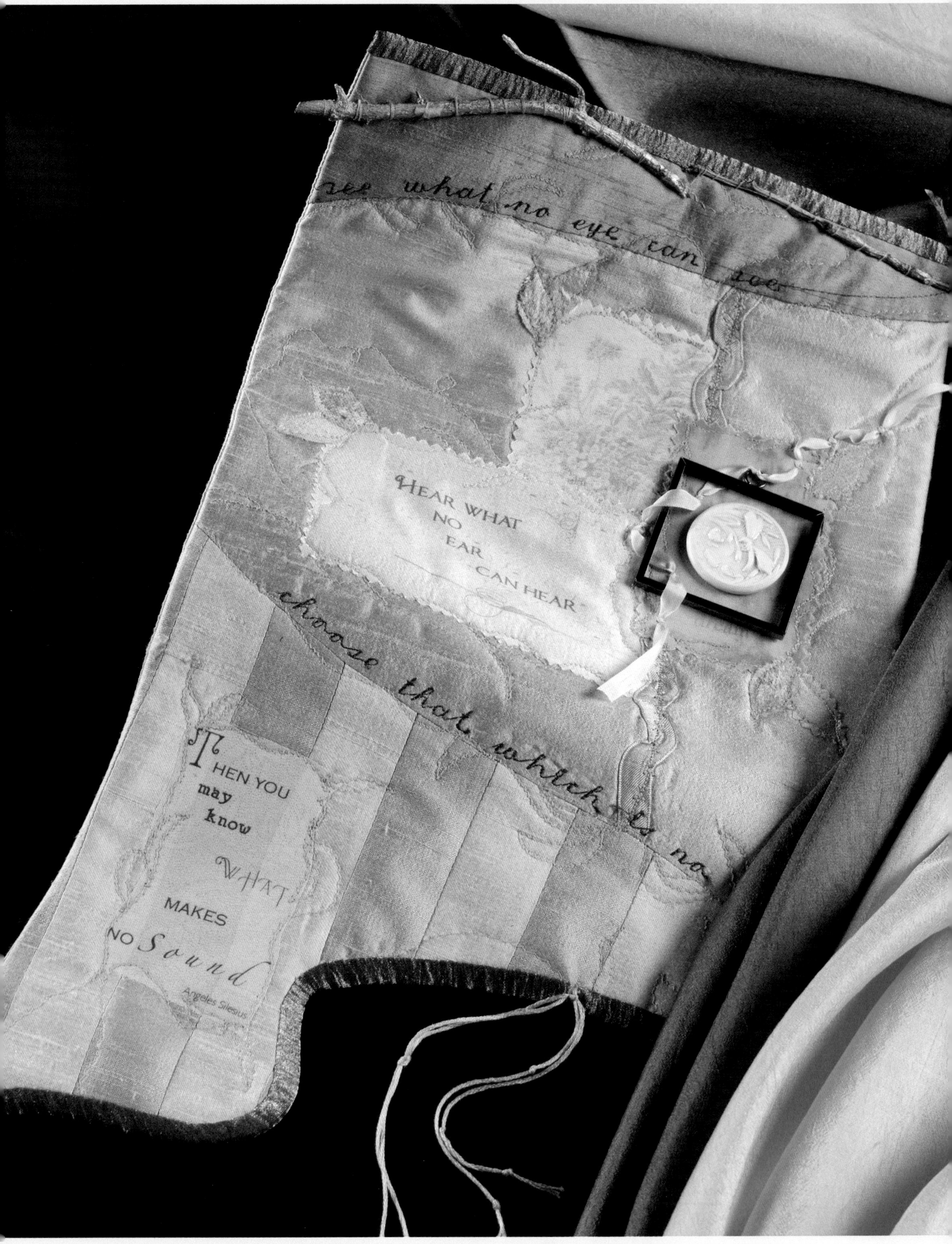

...ee what no eye can ever

qHEAR WHAT
NO
EAR
· CAN HEAR ·

choose that which is no

THEN YOU
may
know
WHAT
MAKES
NO $Sound$

Angeles Silesius

See What No Eye Can See

SEE, HEAR, CHOOSE, KNOW; a portable page of wise advice, perhaps persuading you to realize you are abundantly blessed, graciously filled and sweetly strengthened.

MATERIALS

Silk fabrics:
  10½" x 3½" piece of ocean green dupioni

  10½" x 7½" piece of willow dupioni

  12" x 7½" piece of new fern dupioni

  22" x 7½" piece of daffodil dupioni

  22" x 9" piece of cancun blue dupioni

  6" x 9" piece of maize shantung

  2" x 30" strip of purple/gold metallic crinkle

  6" x 9" piece of off-white silk chiffon

Embellishments:
  Pewter twigs, each about 5" long

  2" x 2" black patina memory frame

  1⁵⁄₁₆"-diameter green Art Stone Dragonfly button

  ½ yd. of 7mm blush silk ribbon

Three small, green velvet leaves

½ yd. of ⅜"-wide aqua with green selvage ribbon

12" each of two different shades of green embroidery floss

Other supplies and tools:
  12" x 16" piece of silk or cotton batting

  1⅛ yd. of 20"-wide lightweight fusible knit interfacing

  Adhesive-backed embroidery stabilizer or freezer paper

  2½" x 3½" piece of paper-backed fusible web

  Brown ink pad suitable for stamping onto fabric

  Sewing machine with machine lettering embroidery ability plus basic accessories

  Sewing threads: neutral or matching

Quilting thread: light khaki

Machine embroidery thread: federal blue and brown

Iron and ironing board
Fabric scissors

Pinking shears

Size 20 chenille needle

Four-color inkjet printer

Desktop publishing software

3-5 sheets of 8½" x 11" all purpose paper

Self-healing cutting mat

Rotary cutter

Grid lined ruler

Pencil

Patterns: See What No Eye Can See A, B, C, D, E, F

Finished size: about 9" x 16"

CUT FABRICS

Cut fabrics, following the chart below. An asterisk indicates the piece is interfaced (*).

Fabric	Description
Ocean green dupioni	Pattern A, cut one
Willow dupioni	Pattern B, cut one
	Pattern G, cut two, using pinking shears
New fern dupioni	Pattern C, cut one
	Backing, cut one 11½" x 3"
	Pattern G, cut two, using pinking shears
Daffodil dupioni	Strips for Pattern D section, cut five 1½" x 8½"
	Backing, cut one 11½" x 7½"
Cancun blue dupioni	Strips for Pattern D section, cut six 1½" x 8½"
	Backing, cut one 11½" x 7½"
Fusible knit interfacing	Cut interfacing for each of the above pieces
	Cut a 6" x 9" piece for maize shantung
	Save scraps for fusing onto chiffon
Adhesive-backed stabilizer	To stabilize silk chiffon, cut one 6" x 9"
	To stabilize maize shantung, cut one 6" x 9"

PIECE FRONT

Seam allowances are ¼" unless otherwise noted.

1 Fuse interfacing to wrong sides of ocean green, willow, new fern, daffodil, cancun blue, chiffon and maize pieces.

2 Sew the 1½"-wide Cancun Blue and Daffodil strips together, alternating shades, right sides facing. Press seam allowances open. Cut the Pattern D piece, right side up, from strip-pieced silk.

3 Sew B to C, right sides facing, matching marked edges. Press seam allowance open. Using a large-sized serpentine stitch, machine gather stitch down the center of the length of ⅜"-wide ribbon. Pull thread to gather ribbon. The serpentine stitch will make the gathered ribbon take on a serpentine shape. Adjust gathers. Pin ribbon centered over B/C seam line. Use a decorative machine stitch to sew ribbon to seam line. Press carefully.

4 Sew A to upper edge of B/C, right sides facing, matching dot on A to B/C seam line. Clip inner curves in order to sew edges together. Press seam allowance open. Sew upper edge of D to lower edge of B/C, right sides facing, matching dot on D to B/C seam line. Clip inner curves before sewing. Press seam allowances open.

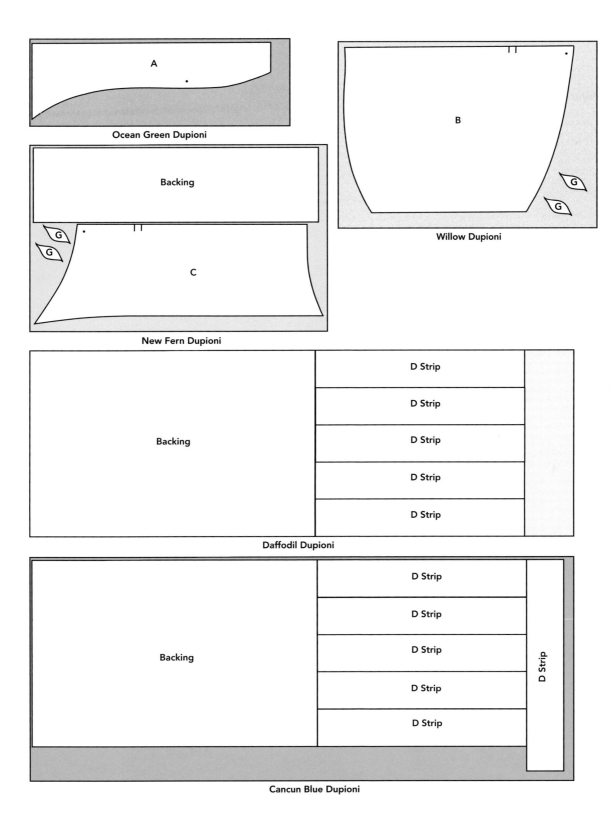

Fabric Cutting Diagrams.

EMBROIDER WORDS

Constructions notes: To determine size and space lettering will require test embroidery on scrap fabric. I used brown thread in the bobbin and federal blue on top. The two shades combined to make a great color for the embroidered words. If machine embroidery is not an option, hand embroidery is an excellent choice.

5 Place paper underneath upper portion of page so that it is centered under seam line. Embroider the sentence: "See What No Eye Can See," placing lettering a scant amount above seam line. Begin lettering about ⅜" inward from left side edge and at end of this first sentence, switch to straight sewing and trail off page with stitching. Tear paper away. Press.

6 With paper underneath lower portion of page, embroider the sentence: "choose that which is no choice," placing lettering again a scant amount above the seam line. Begin lettering about 1½" inward from left side edge. Tear paper away. Press.

PRINT IMAGES

With regard to printing images on silk chiffon, you have several alternatives. Purchase silk chiffon that already is paper-backed, scan and print the images on page 122 from your home computer and inkjet printer; or design your own image and print onto the silk chiffon. Another alternative is to purchase the images pre-printed onto silk. Refer to the author's page for more information on how to purchase pre-printed images. The directions below assume you will need to prepare the chiffon for printing.

7 Apply adhesive-backed stabilizer or quilter's freezer paper to interfaced side of maize dupioni and off-white chiffon. Using rotary cutter, self-healing cutting mat and grid lined ruler, trim both pieces to 5½" x 8½", making certain that none of the adhesive from stabilizer is exposed.

8 Scan "Hear What No Ear Can Hear" on page 122 and place into 5½" x 8½" sized file in the desktop publishing program on your computer. Print image onto a sheet of paper to test results. Then, place stabilized piece of maize shantung into your printer, either face up or down, depending on printer requirements. Print image onto the silk. Let ink dry. Remove stabilizer, but not interfacing. Press. Trace pattern E centered over printed image. Cut out, using pinking shears.

9 Scan "Makes No Sound," "Forget Me Nots," and "Sky" images on page 122. Place into 5½" x 8½" sized file in the desktop publishing file program on your computer. Print onto piece of chiffon following step 8. Don't forget to test first on a sheet of paper..

10 Trace pattern F centered onto "Sky" and "Forget Me Nots" image. Cut out, using pinking shears.

11 Fuse paper-backed adhesive web to wrong side of chiffon underneath "Makes No Sound" image. Trim image close to outer edges of lettering.

12 Pin the three printed images onto upper section of page. Fuse "Makes No Sound" image to lower section of page along the left side.

Construction notes: Aging the velvet leaves can be accomplished using several techniques. For this project's velvet leaves, I tapped the brown ink pad lightly onto the leaves, then misted them with water, blending the ink into the leaves with my fingers.

13 Age the velvet leaves. Press dry. Pin the velvet and silk leaves to the upper section printed images near some of the corners.

QUILT AND FINISH

14 Sew daffodil backing piece to new fern backing piece along one 11½" edge, right sides facing. Sew cancun blue backing piece to remaining 11½" new fern edge, right sides facing. Press seam allowances open.

15 Layer batting underneath page front. Machine quilt front with a small meandering leaf pattern accomplished with the free-motion quilting technique, sewing all individual elements in place in the process. Use the khaki thread for the task. Place all purpose paper on the batting side before quilting and tear away once quilting is complete.

Construction notes: The sewing machine I used has a stitch regulator for free-motion quilting or embroidery, which allows me to use either a straight stitch and a zigzag stitch. I used the zigzag stitch option to create the free-motion embroidery design. If your machine does not have the zigzag stitch option, use the straight stitch to machine quilt the meandering leaf pattern with the free-motion technique. Test your movements and thread on scrap fabric to get a feel for the free-motion design.

16 Pin front to backing, right sides facing. Trim batting and backing to match front size and shape. Sew front to back along side edges. Edge press seam allowance open. Turn right side out. Press flat, lightly, from backing side.

17 For binding, press the purple/gold metallic crinkle in half, matching long edges. Sew binding to top and bottom edges, right sides facing. At edges, fold ends over to backing, then fold binding over onto backing, enclosing seam allowances. Hand sew binding in place.

18 Hand sew frame over "Sky" and "Forget Me Nots" image, using the 7mm silk ribbon and the cascading stitch. Center button within frame and sew on. Hand sew pewter twigs to top edge of page. Sew embroidery floss to bottom edge of page, working the two shades as one. Tie knots along length of floss.

Cascading Stitch Diagram.

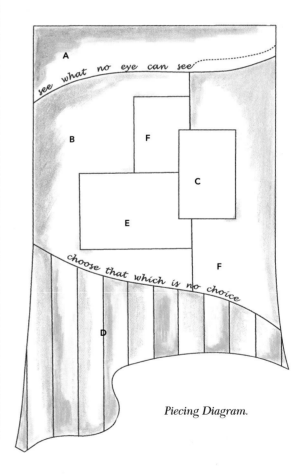

Piecing Diagram.

Favorite Things

AS A LITTLE GIRL, I would accompany my mom on her fabric shopping excursions. A favorite store displayed a dress form in their window cleverly draped with a length of fabric that suggested a garment. Many years later in college, I took garment-draping classes. I've always loved the shape of a dress form. For me, it conjures up the promise of unlimited possibilities. This Portable Page represents a myriad of favorite things: fabrics, trims, sketches, angels and many simple statements that help us to be grateful for another beautiful day.

MATERIALS

Silk fabrics:
  12" x 15" piece of light-pink dupioni

  9" x 11" piece of wood dupioni

  9" x 11" piece of mocha shantung

  6" x 6" piece of bright-pink dupioni (dress form)

  1⅝" x 1½" scrap of medium-pink noil (silk color card)

  8" x 13" piece of off-white organza

  5½" x 8½" piece of off-white jacquard (printed specialty pieces)

Embellishments:
  1¼ yd. of ⅜"-wide cream/brown jacquard ribbon

  ½ yd. of 7mm taupe silk ribbon

  Assorted bits of pink and brown trims to wrap around trim card

18" of mocha embroidery floss

Three ⅝"-wide blush colored hand painted glass buttons

Dress form rubber stamp

Wings rubber stamp

Black and brown ink pad, suitable for stamping onto fabric

Fine point black and brown permanent ink pen

Other supplies and tools:
  Adhesive-backed embroidery stabilizer

  8" x 18" piece of silk or cotton batting

  7½" x 18" piece of fusible knit interfacing

  8½" x 8½" piece of paper-backed fusible web

  4" scrap of poster board

  Transparent tape

  Iron and ironing board

  Basic sewing supplies

Sewing machine with basic machine embroidery ability plus basic accessories

Self-healing cutting mat

Rotary cutter

Acrylic ruler

Pencil

Threads: Neutral or matching, plus medium pink for machine embroidery

Scissors, fabric and craft

Pinking shears

Size 20 chenille needle

Four-color inkjet printer

Desktop Publishing Software

Favorite Things Patterns: Envelope

Image of Favorite Things backdrop to print onto silk

Image of specialty frames and dress sketch to print onto silk

Finished size: 8" x 14½"

CUT FABRICS

Cut fabrics, following the chart below.

Fabric	Description	Cut size
Light pink dupioni	Top binding	1¾" x 9"
	Backdrop	7½" x 15"
Wood dupioni	Backing	7¼" x 10½"
	Silk color card	1⅝" x 1½"
Mocha shantung	Lower binding	1¾" x 9"
	Backing	7¼" x 10½"
	Silk color card	1⅝" x 1½"
Off-white organza	Envelope	8" x 10"
	For wings (this piece is torn)	2¼" x 4½"
Bright pink dupioni	For stamped dress form	3" x 6" (cut 2)
Interfacing	Backdrop	7½" x 15"
	Printed specialty pieces	5½" x 8½"
	For stamped dress form	3" x 6"
Stabilizer	Backdrop	7½" x 15"
	Printed specialty pieces	5½" x 8½"
Fusible web	Printed specialty pieces	5¼" x 8¼"
	Silk color card	1⅝" x 1½" (cut 3)
Silk or cotton batting	For page	8" x 14"
	For dress form	3" x 6"

The individual specialty elements are printed or stamped onto silk before making this Portable Page. The elements include the printed backdrop, printed specialty frames and dress sketch, organza envelope, stamped dress form and wings. The directions below assume you will not need to prepare the silks for printing or stamping.

PRINT THE BACKDROP

Scan "Favorite Things" backdrop, page 123, and place into a 6½" x 14" sized page in the desktop publishing program on your computer. Please note that the scanned image is to be enlarged 200 percent.

An alternative is to purchase the image pre-printed onto silk. Refer to the author's page for more information on how to purchase pre-printed images.

1 Fuse interfacing to wrong side of light pink dupioni for backdrop. Apply adhesive-backed stabilizer to the interfaced side of dupioni. Using rotary cutter, self-healing cutting mat and grid lined ruler, trim backdrop piece to 6½" x 14", making certain that none of the adhesive from the stabilizer is exposed.

2 Print "Favorite Things" backdrop image, page 123. Print the file onto a sheet of paper to test results. Then, place stabilized piece of light pink silk dupioni into your printer, either face up or down, depending on printer requirements. Print file onto the silk. Let ink dry. An alternative is to purchase the image pre-printed onto silk, see page 127.

PRINT SPECIALTY PIECES

The lower portion of the portable page is embellished with a "silk fabric color card," "trim color card," "angel message" and "dress sketch." Each of these images is printed onto the piece of off-white silk jacquard fabric. Scan the image from page 123 and place into a 5½" x 8½" file in the desktop publishing program on your computer.

Silks color and trim cards.

3 Scan the images on page 124 and place in a 5½" x 8½" sized page in your desktop publishing software. Fuse interfacing to wrong side of off-white jacquard. Apply adhesive-backed stabilizer to the interfaced side of jacquard. Using rotary cutter, self-healing cutting mat and grid lined ruler, trim backdrop piece to 5¼" x 8¼", making certain none of the stabilizer adhesive is exposed.

4 Print the file onto a sheet of paper to test results. Then, place stabilized piece of jacquard into your printer, either face up or down, depending on printer requirements. Print file onto the silk. Let ink dry. An alternative would be to purchase images pre-printed onto silk.

EMBELLISH THE SPECIALTY PIECES

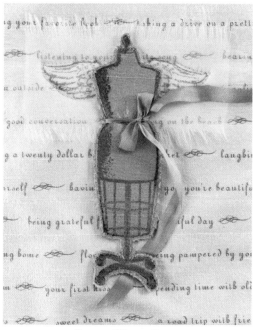

Stamped Dress Form.

5 Remove the stabilizer from backside of the jacquard. Press jacquard. Apply fusible web to backside of jacquard. Trim "Silk" color card and angel message frame from jacquard close to outer edge of images. Trim dress sketch from jacquard with a bit of excess around image. For the trim color card, apply a piece of fusible web to wrong side of frame, then fuse to scrap of poster board. If desired, you can fuse a scrap of fabric over poster board. Trim color card from excess jacquard close to outer edge of image.

6 Apply fusible web to backsides of wood, mocha and medium-pink Silk color card pieces. Fuse pieces layered to Silk color card frame. Wrap trim color card with assorted bits of brown and pink lace and ribbon, taping ends to backside of card.

MAKE ENVELOPE

7 Press 8" x 10" piece of off-white organza in half, matching 8" edges. Trace envelope onto one side of pressed organza, using pencil. Sew around envelope on traced line, using the serpentine stitch, with very narrow width and a length of .08mm. Trim sewn envelope from organza as close to stitching as possible, using pinking shears.

8 Press envelope sides over and bottom flap upward on dashed lines indicated on pattern. Hand sew overlapping edges together.

STAMP DRESS FORM AND WINGS

9 Apply interfacing to one 3" x 6" bright-pink dupioni piece. Place bright-pink dupioni, face-up, on a piece of cardboard, such as the back from a pad of paper. Ink dress form rubber stamp with the brown and black fabric inks. Press inked stamp onto right side of interfaced silk (test first on scrap paper/fabric to get a feel for the process). Heat set image with iron. Use permanent ink pens to deepen lines of stamped image. Heat set.

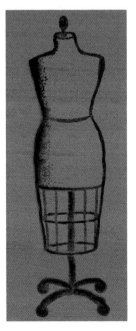

Image of dress form stamped onto fabric, with pen-deepened detail lines.

10 Place 3" x 6" batting between stamped and other bright pink dupioni, wrong sides facing. Sew layers together as close to outer edge of stamped image as possible. Trim excess fabric close to stitching.

11 Place torn organza piece on work surface. Ink the wing stamps with a combination of the brown and black fabric inks, as was done for dress form. Press inked stamps onto organza, spacing them to be just behind the dress form shoulders when the dress form image is placed in front of the wings. Heat set wings and deepen images a bit with the permanent ink pens.

CREATE THE PAGE

12 Pin grouping of Silk color card, envelope, angel message frame and dress sketch on the lower half of the front piece. Envelope is about 1½" upward from lower edge. Fray all edges of the organza wings piece. Pin centered to upper half of front so that wings are about 2" down from top edge.

13 Sew wood and mocha backing pieces together, right sides facing, matching 10½" edges, using a ¼" seam allowance. Press seam allowance open.

14 Center front onto 8" x 14" batting and pin.

15 Pin and sew long edges of backing to layered front/batting, right sides facing, using a ¼" seam allowance. Turn right side out and press lightly.

16 Machine quilt close to edge of specialty items on lower half of page, but do not quilt through envelope. Machine quilt around image of stamped wings, leaving torn edges free. Machine quilt page sides using a decorative machine embroidery stitch and pink thread.

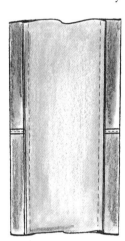

Sew backing to long edges of front/batting, right sides facing. Turn right side out.

FINISHING TOUCHES

17 Press binding strips in half, matching long edges. Sew raw edges of light pink binding to top edge of page, right sides facing. Sew mocha binding to lower edge of page, right sides facing. At lower edge, fold binding ends over to backing side, then fold bottom edge up on backing side, enclosing lower seam allowance. Hand sew binding in place.

18 At top edge, fold and pin binding ends over to backing side. Cut three 3" lengths from cream-brown ribbon. Fold each length in half, matching cut ends. Pin loop ends to top edge on backing side, then fold upper binding edge down, enclosing seam allowance. Hand sew binding to backing, sewing loops in place at the same time.

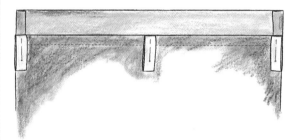

Pin ribbon loops to top edge of page along seam allowance on backing side.

19 Fold ribbon loops upward and hand sew onto top binding.

20 Pin dress form to front with shoulders centered between wings. Sew to front at top and bottom. Thread 7mm ribbon into chenille needle and sew through page at dress form waist. Tie ribbon snugly into a bow. Drape ribbon ends, tacking them in place.

21 Sew the three buttons to lower edge of page. Cut three 10" lengths from cream/brown ribbon. Tie each length around buttons. Trim ends at a slant.

Reflections True and Noble

WHENEVER I HEAR OR READ SOMETHING or have an idea that plucks my inner heart strings, I write or sketch the inspiration on the nearest surface, whether it's my lunch napkin or the latest phone message sheet. A wiser choice would be a silk-covered book, one that will envelope lofty thoughts.

MATERIALS

Silk fabrics:
  1½" x 9½" strip of tan oak silk dupioni

  1½" x 9½" strip of grasshopper silk dupioni

  1½" x 9½" strip of kiwi silk dupioni

  1½" x 9½" strip of ocean green silk dupioni

  5¼" x 9½" strip of lime silk dupioni

  5¼" x 9½" strip of lavender blue silk dupioni

  9" x 11" piece of curry silk dupioni

Other supplies and tools:
  5" x 7" journal with ¾" spine

  7" x 11" piece of silk or cotton batting or fusible fleece

  7" piece of ¾" vintage tatting scrap

  ⅝ yd. of 20" lightweight fusible knit interfacing

  8½" x 11" sheet of paper-backed cotton

  Inkjet printer

  Word Processor

Iron and ironing board

Sewing machine plus basic accessories

Basic sewing supplies

Self-healing cutting mat

Rotary cutter

Grid lined ruler

Sewing Threads: neutral or matching

Finished size: Covers have been designed for either a 5" x 7" or 7" x 9" journal or sketchbook

CUT FABRICS

Fabric	Description	Cut size
Lime dupioni	Horizontal band	1½" x 9½"
	Back vertical strip and inner sleeve	3¾" x 7½"
Lavender blue dupioni	Horizontal band	1½" x 9½"
	Front vertical strip and inner sleeve	3¾" x 7½"
Curry dupioni	Horizontal band	1½" x 9½"
	Jacket lining	7½" x 11"
Lightweight, fusible knit interfacing	Interfacing	7 strips 1½" x 9½"
		2 pieces 3¾" x 7½"
		1 piece 7½" x 11"

1 The tan oak, grasshopper, kiwi and ocean green strips are already cut to size, according to the materials list.

2 Place all like-sized strips and pieces together.

3 Fuse interfacing to the seven 1½" x 9½" silk strips, to the two 3¾" x 7½" silk pieces and the one 7½" x 11" silk piece.

SEW COVER FRONTS

Seam allowances are ¼" unless otherwise noted.

4 Sew the 1½" x 9½" strips together following the diagram, forming a horizontally-striped piece. Press seam allowances open.

For Reflections True and Noble cover, sew together the 1½"-wide strips, forming a horizontally striped piece, then sew side pieces.

5 Sew the 3¾" x 7½" lavender blue front vertical strip/inner sleeve piece to the right edge of the striped piece, right sides facing, matching the 7½" edges. Sew the 3¾" x 7½" lime back vertical strip and inner sleeve piece to the left edge. Press seam allowances open.

6 Hand sew the scrap of tatted lace to the right edge seamline that is between the horizontally-striped piece and vertical front side.

MAKE LABELS

7 Working with a computer, word processor and new file (oriented landscape), type journal title onto page, using a font style of choice. Font size will vary, depending on type used. I suggest testing sizes 18–24. Print test on paper. Trim paper labels so they are ½" wide and place centered onto spine area of cover front to determine if the font and size chosen is going to work. Continue testing if necessary. When pleased with type font and size, print onto the paper-backed cotton. Trim fabric labels so they are ½" wide and save the rest of the paper-backed cotton for another project.

8 Peel paper back from printed cotton label. Center label onto spine or center of cover front. Sew in place, using a machine decora-

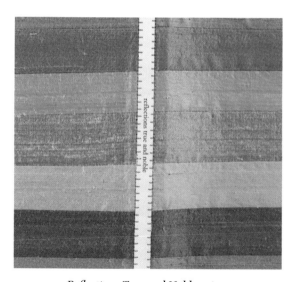

Reflections True and Noble spine.

9 Sew a ¼" doubled hem along the remaining long edges of both side pieces. Press.

10 Pin or fuse batting or fleece centered to wrong side of front. Batting or fleece will not extend onto inner sleeves. If desired, quilt front by machine or by hand.

11 Fold both side and inner sleeve edges over 2" onto front, right sides facing. Pin in place.

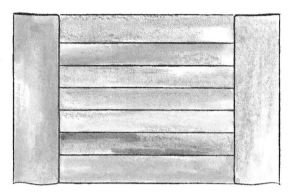

Fold inner sleeve edges over 2" onto front.

FINISH COVER

12 Pin lining piece to front, right sides facing, aligning all edges. Sew top and bottom edges. At bottom, leave a 3 opening in order to turn cover right side out. Edge press seam allowances open. Turn right side out through opening. Press.

13 Slip journal front and back cover into inner sleeves.

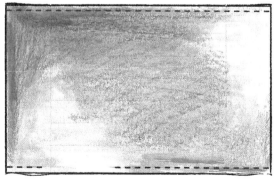

Sew lining to front along top and bottom edges, leaving an opening along bottom for turning cover right side out.

Heart Etchings Cover

MATERIALS

Silk fabrics:

5" x 9⅝" strip of coral silk noil

8¼" x 9⅝" strip of copper silk dupioni

1¾" x 9¼" strip of curry silk dupioni

6½" x 9⅝" strip of persimmon silk dupioni

1¼" x 9¼" strip of pumpkin silk dupioni

11½" x 15" piece of poppy silk dupioni

2⅛" x 9¼" piece of azalea silk dupioni

Other supplies and tools:

7" x 9" journal with ¾" spine

9⅛" x 15" piece of silk or cotton batting or fusible fleece

9¼" pieces of seven different vintage lace trims. Trims range in width from ¼" to 2¼" and are a variety of lace types

¾ yd. of 20" lightweight fusible knit interfacing

8½" x 11" sheet of paper-backed cotton

Inkjet printer

Word Processor

Iron and ironing board

Sewing machine plus basic accessories

Basic sewing supplies

Self-healing cutting mat

Rotary cutter

Grid lined ruler

Sewing Threads: neutral or matching

For the Heart Etchings cover, cut fabrics as shown in the chart below and cut one piece of interfacing to match each fabric cut size.

Fabric	Description	Cut size	Fabric	Description	Cut size
Coral noil	Horizontal band	1⅞" x 9¼"		Back strip	5" x 9⅝"
	Inner sleeve	2¾" x 9⅝"	Pumpkin dupioni	Horizontal band	1¼" x 9¼"
Copper dupioni	Horizontal band	3⅛" x 9¼"	Poppy dupioni	Horizontal band	1⅜" x 9¼"
	Back strip and inner sleeve	4¾" x 9⅝"		Jacket lining	9⅝" x 15"
Curry dupioni	Horizontal band	1¾" x 9¼"	Azalea dupioni	Horizontal band	2⅛" x 9¼"
Persimmon dupioni	Horizontal band	1⅛" x 9¼"			

1 Sew the 9¼" to different-width strips together following the diagram, forming the horizontally-striped front band. Press seam allowances open.

2 Sew the various lace trims to the horizontal band along seam lines.

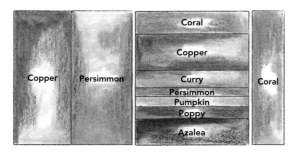

For Heart Etchings cover, sew the different-width strips together, forming a horizontally-striped band. Trim with laces and sew side pieces.

3 Sew the Coral 2¾" x 9⅝" inner sleeve piece to the right edge of the horizontal band, right sides facing. Sew the Persimmon 5" x 9⅝" back piece to the left edge of the horizontal band, right sides facing. Sew the Copper 4¾" x 9⅝" back/inner sleeve piece to the left side of the Persimmon piece, right sides facing. Press seam allowances open.

4 Continue with steps 7-13 in "Reflections True and Noble" to complete.

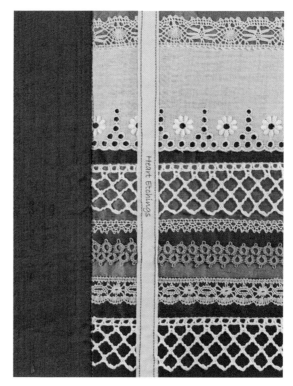

Heart Etchings spine.

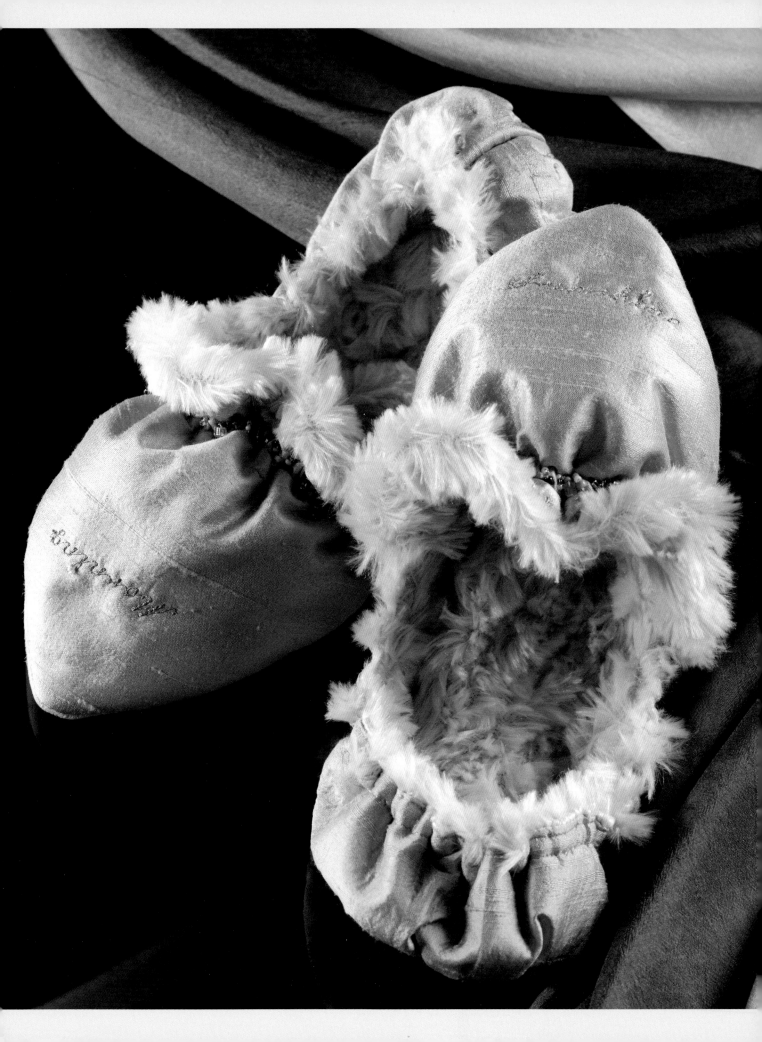

Creature Comforts

A PAIR OF SOFT, ELEGANT AND WARM SILK SLIPPERS is a lovely gift to make. The slippers are quilted using wool batting, which is extremely lightweight and very soft. The slippers can be made in small (5-6), medium (7-8) or large (9-10) women's sizes. If you are so inclined, a message can be added to the slippers.

MATERIALS

For the Mauve Slippers, all sizes

Silk fabrics:

¼ yd. mauve silk taffeta for top

¼ yd. antique gold silk dupioni for side back

⅜ yd. dusty purple silk dupioni for Lining (inner sole, top, side back)

Other supplies and tools:

6" x 26" taupe-grey shaggy suede for outer sole

12 ¼" x 11" muslin for quilted inner sole backing

⅓ yd. 44" wool batting

⅜ yd. of 1" plum hand-dyed bias cut silk ribbon

Sewing machine plus basic accessories and darning foot

Size 11/0 bronze and mauve seed beads (about 75 altogether, or mixed package of beads)

For the Morning Sunshine Slippers, all sizes

Silk fabrics:

9" x 22" new fern silk dupioni for top

9" x 22" aqua silk dupioni for side back

Other supplies and tools:

⅜ yd. mint green minky plush swirl for lining (inner sole, top, side back)

6" x 26" mint green shaggy suede for outer sole

9" x 22" silk, cotton or wool batting

Mixed package of blue and green small-sized beads

Sewing machine with basic machine embroidery lettering ability plus basic accessories

Machine embroidery threads: bright blue

Machine embroidery needle

Scrap sheet of paper

Both slippers, all sizes

Other supplies and tools:

1 yd. of ¼"-wide elastic

5½" x 24" of 44" fusible fleece

⅔ yd. 20" lightweight knit fusible interfacing

Ball-point bodkin

Fabric scissors

Iron and ironing board

Machine needles: sizes 12 and 14

Other needles, hand, milliners (or beading)

Sewing threads: neutral or matching

Slipper patterns: A, B, C (small, medium, large), D, E

Mauve Slippers
CUTTING GUIDE

Transfer all sewing construction markings.

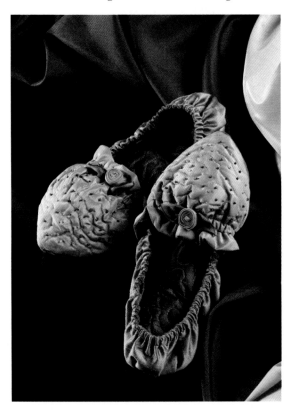

Fabric	Pattern	Description	Quantity
Mauve silk taffeta	B	Top	Cut two ½" larger as indicated on pattern to allow for quilting (one left, one right)
	E	Coiled rose	Cut 2 on the bias
Antique gold dupioni	C	Side back	Cut 2 along the fold
Dusty purple dupioni	B	Top (lining)	Cut two ½" larger as indicated on pattern (one left, one right)
	C	Side back (lining)	Cut 2 along fold
	D	Inner sole	Cut one 12¼" x 11"
Shaggy suede	A	Sole	Cut 2 (one left, one right)
Fusible interfacing	B	Top	Cut two ½" larger as indicated on pattern (one left, one right)
	C	Side back	Cut 2 along fold
	D	Inner sole	Cut one 12¼" x 11"
Batting	B	Top	Cut two ½" larger as indicated on pattern (one left, one right)
	D	Inner sole	Cut one 12¼" x 11"
Fusible fleece	A	Top	Cut two ⅜" smaller all around the pattern (one left, one right)

Fuse the interfacing to the wrong side of each mauve Top piece, each antique gold Side back piece and the 12¼" x 11" dusty purple piece for inner Sole.

QUILT THE INNER SOLES

1 Quilt the fabrics for the inner Sole by layering the wool batting between the wrong sides of the muslin and lining pieces. Use the free-motion method to quilt the layers.

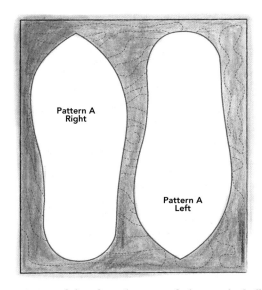

Step 2: Cut 1 left and 1 right inner sole from quilted silk.

2 Cut out 1 left and 1 right inner Sole from the quilted piece.

3 Fuse the Sole pieces cut from the fusible fleece to the muslin side of the inner Soles.

SEW THE TOP

Use a ⅜" seam allowance unless otherwise noted. When sewing, remember that you are making two slippers, one for the left foot and one for the right.

4 Pin the Top and Top lining pieces together with right sides facing while layering the wool batting underneath the wrong side of the lining.

5 Sew the ruffle edge. Trim batting from seam allowance as close to the seam line as possible. Edge press and turn right side out. Press from lining side. Pin the layers together for easier control.

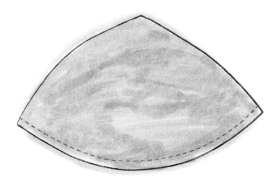

Step 5: Sew top ruffle edge and trim batting from seam allowance.

6 Working from top right side, sew casing space indicated on the pattern.

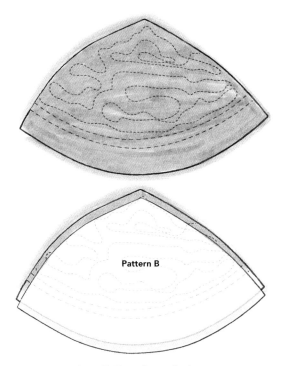

Step 7: Trim the quilted top.

7 Quilt layers, using the free-motion method, but do not quilt through casing space or along ruffle area. Once quilted, trim to size, using pattern B. Remember to subtract for seam allowance along ruffle edge when trimming.

8 Use the bodkin tool to slip a length of elastic through casing. Pin elastic at outer edges of casing and then machine sew ends in place. Use the following measurements for elastic, adjusting as necessary to suit personal fit:

Small: 4½"
Medium: 5"
Large: 5½"

9 If desired, Tops can be beaded at this point, or you can wait until the slippers are finished.

SEW THE SIDE BACK

10 Pin Side back and Side back lining pieces together with right sides facing. Sew the casing edge. Edge press and turn right side out. Press flat from lining side.

Step 10: Sew Side back casing edge.

11 Sew casing space by stitching ⅜" inward from finished edge. Staystitch the remaining edges together, but do not stitch through casing space at edge.

12 Slip a length of elastic through casing, pinning elastic at the outer edges and sewing ends in place. Use the following measurements for elastic, adjusting as necessary to suit personal taste:

Small: 10–11"
Medium: 11–12"
Large: 12–13"

SEW THE TOP, SIDE BACK TO INNER SOLE

13 Pin Side back to inner Sole, lining sides facing, aligning Side back ends to stars shown on pattern. Clip Side backs to stay stitching as needed. Where Side back will be sewn to heel, hand gather-stitch Side back along space indicated on pattern. Pull gathering thread as tightly as necessary in order for Side back to fit heel area on inner Sole. Secure thread and pin gathers in place.

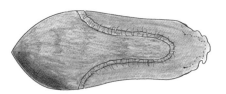

Step 13: Hand gather-stitch heel space on Side back.

14 Pin top to inner sole, lining sides facing, aligning "ruffle" ends to side dots on soles shown on pattern. The top is overlapped onto side back. Sew top and side back to inner sole.

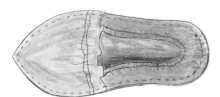

Step 14: Overlap Top onto Side back, sew to inner Sole.

SEW THE SOLE

15 Pin Top and Side back so they are flat against the inner Sole in order to keep those parts away from the sole seam line.

16 Pin and sew right side of outer Sole to right side of the inner Sole/Top/Side back, breaking stitches to leave opening indicated by squares on Sole pattern.

17 Trim inner Sole seam allowance to a scant ⅛". Trim outer Sole seam allowance to a generous ⅛".

18 Turn slipper right side out through opening. Push out seam lines. Hand sew opening closed.

FINISHING TOUCHES

19 Hand sew seed beads individually to Tops (see Special Techniques on page 9).

20 Make 2 folded leaves from ribbon (see Folded Leaf Technique on page 61). Sew leaves to Top centered over casing.

21 Fold Coiled Rose bias strip in half, matching long edges. Sew long edges, using a ¼" seam allowance. Turn right side out, using bodkin tool, forming a length of spaghetti. Use fingertips to flatten spaghetti.

Step 21: Use the bodkin tool to turn sewn bias right side out.

22 Tie a knot at one end of the spaghetti. Hand sew end underneath knot. Coil spaghetti around knot, hand sewing coils in place on underside, forming a small, tailored rose. Sew rose centered over leaves.

Step 22: Coil flattened spaghetti around center knot.

Morning Sunshine Slippers
CUTTING GUIDE

1 Cut fabrics, following the cutting guide below.

Transfer all sewing construction markings.

Fabric	Pattern	Description	Quantity
New fern dupioni	B	Top	Cut 2 (one left, one right)
Aqua dupioni	C	Side and back	Cut 2 along fold
Mint green minky	A	Inner sole	Cut 2 (one left, one right)
	B	Inner top	Cut 2 (one left, one right)
	C	Inner side and back	Cut 2 along fold
Mint green shaggy	A	Bottom sole	Cut 2 (one left, one right)
Batting	B	Top	Cut two ½" larger all around than pattern (one left, one right)
Fusible fleece	A	Sole	Cut two ⅜" smaller all around than pattern (one left, one right)
Fusible interfacing	B	Top	Cut two (one left, one right)
	C	Side back	Cut two along fold

2 Fuse fleece to wrong sides of each mint green minky sole. Fuse interfacing to wrong sides of each new fern dupioni top and each aqua dupioni Side/back.

EMBROIDER THE TOP

Embroidery and beaded slipper.

Constructions notes: Each top is embroidered near the toes with "Morning" and "Sunshine". To determine the size and space the lettering will require, test embroidery on scrap fabric. When ready to embroider the slipper tops, place the lettering centered between the top sides. Test embroidery designs to sew along the ruffle edge as well. If machine embroidery is not possible with your sewing machine, hand embroidery is an excellent option.

3 Pin batting to wrong sides of each Top piece. Place paper underneath batting. Using your sewing machine's lettering capabilities, machine embroider the word "Morning" on the upper left Top and "Sunshine" on the upper right Top. Tear paper away from batting side.

4 Machine embroider Tops along the ruffle edge, placing stitches about ⅝" inward from outer curved edge.

SEW THE TOP

Use a ⅜" seam allowance unless otherwise noted. When sewing remember that you are making two slippers, one for the left foot and one for the right. After a seam has been sewn, pick the minky out from the seam line for a fluffy edge.

5 Sew the Top and inner Tops together, right sides facing, along ruffle edge. Edge press and turn right side out and press. Sew casing space indicated on pattern. Insert elastic into casing (see step 8 for mauve slippers on page 39).

SEW THE SIDE BACK

6 Pin and sew side/back to inner side back, as with steps 10 – 12 for the mauve slippers on page 40.

SEW THE TOP, SIDE BACK TO INNER SOLE

7 Continue as with steps 13–14 for mauve slippers on page 40.

SEW THE SOLE

8 Continue as with steps 15–18 for mauve slippers on page 41.

FINISHING TOUCHES

9 Hand-sew clusters of seed beads to Tops along casing space.

CHAPTER 3

The Unexpected Quilt

I HAVE ALWAYS LOVED SIMPLE, GEOMETRIC QUILTS and ample patterns are available for such. But what about the unexpected quilt, a surprising composition, what would that look like?

An unexpected quilt could Ignore the Rules with a slightly off-beat rectangular shape or be an example of texture as in Gathering Warmth. I think an unexpected quilt could represent something from A Poet's Garden or be a Wildly Charming garment. An unexpected quilt could be Almost Famous, serving two purposes, one useful and one decorative. What if an unexpected quilt inspired you to Spread Your Wings or prove you are a Natural Beauty?

I want to tell you a little story. My sewing machines have been good friends. Do you feel like this? It's silly, isn't it, to feel so close to a machine. I had the same sewing machine for about 20 years, a little Bernina Minimatic that I bought myself. That machine helped me make those four Carmen Miranda costumes that I had to finish a few weeks before my wedding. We were both treading ruffles. My machine helped me sew my wedding dress, was there at the birth of our three kids, moved with us into too many apartments and houses and kept sewing—even after the motor burned out two times. When I did finally get a new machine, I gave my Minimatic to my sister and I cried saying goodbye. It's not just a machine, it's a reliable friend and confidant, listening to your woes and helping you achieve your dreams…if it could talk, it would tell you a story—an unexpected story.

Ignore the Rules

THE ART NOUVEAU AND ART DECO time periods have always appealed to me, more than any other really, from a design perspective. The clothing, the graphic images, the hairdo's, the colors, the design lines beg for an opportunity to visit this moment in time. Ignore the Rules depicts the flourishing softness of Art Nouveau as it meets the strength and boldness of Art Deco in a not-quite-so-rectangular art quilt. Placed between these two frames lies the silhouette of a woman. So many fashionable ladies could have stood between the burgeoning gestures and the confident patterns.

MATERIALS

Note: Refer to Fabric Key on page 54 and 56.

Silk fabrics for Art Deco blocks:
Darks (44" goods)

⅝ yd. russet dupioni (also used for backing)

⅜ yd. brown geometric print

⅜ yd. black geometric print

⅜ yd. brown shadow dupioni (also used for Binding)

Lights (44" goods)

⅜ yd. cream with tan wave print

1⅜ yd. fawn dupioni (also used for backing, woman's face and hands)

1 yd. lavender blush dupioni (also used for backing)

⅜ yd. light maize dupioni

½ yd. muslin for Art Deco dummy blocks

Silk fabrics for Art Nouveau appliquéd flourishes (44" goods unless otherwise noted):
¼ yd. dusty purple jacquard (also used for binding)

½ yd. 28"–30" dusty lavender brocade (also used for binding and rod pocket)

¼ yd. orange/rust chiffon burnout

¼ yd. 28"–30" burgundy brocade

¼ yd. plum dupioni

¼ yd. dusty burgundy geometric jacquard (also used for Binding)

⅓ yd. Heliotrope linen-weave with slubs

¼ yd. pistachio dupioni

Silk fabric for 1920s lady:
⅓ yd. coffee bean dupioni (also used for binding)

Embellishments:
Ribbons for bouquet:
½ yd. of ⅝" dark lavender cross dyed

5" of ⅝" lavender ombré

5" of 1" red orange bias cut silk

7½" of 1" dusty purple bias cut silk

½ yd. of ⅜" dusty purple grosgrain (also used for lady's hat)

½ yd. of 7mm dusty purple silk ribbon (for bow)

Beads:
Fourteen 3mm plum round beads (lady's bodice and shoes)

7 assorted, weird 8mm–12mm beads (for dangles)

About seventy-five 8mm or larger assorted seed beads (for dangles)

15 large old gold sequins (Art Deco blocks)

15 plum seed beads 11mm (Art Deco blocks)

Other supplies and tools:
11 yd. of 20" white or ivory lightweight, fusible knit interfacing

½ yd. of 20"-wide black lightweight fusible knit interfacing (for orange/rust chiffon burnout)

36" x 64" piece of silk or cotton batting

Quilter's freezer paper (this is optional or as needed)

Iron and ironing board

Sewing machine with basic machine embroidery ability plus basic accessories

Darning foot for free motion quilting

Basic sewing supplies

Self-healing cutting mat

Rotary cutter

Grid lined ruler

Scissors, fabric and craft

Sewing threads: neutral and matching

Machine embroidery threads: black, plum, light gold

Pencil

Masking tape

Patterns

Art Deco blocks: A, B, C, D, X, Y, Z.

Art Nouveau Flourishes: #1, 2, 3, 4, 5, 6, 7, 8, 9, 10, 11, 12, 13, 14, 15, 16, 17, 18, 19, 20, 21, 22.

1920s Lady: A, B, C, D, E, F, G, H, I, J

Finished size: 32" x 60"

STABILIZE THE SILKS

Before cutting out the Art Deco block pieces and the Art Nouveau flourishes, fusible knit interfacing is applied to the fabric backsides. Cut the parts first that do not require interfacing. Then, apply interfacing to the silk pieces prior to cutting the parts that do require interfacing. For many of the fabrics, it will not be necessary to interface the entire piece of silk. If your fabric of choice is cotton, interfacing is not needed.

CUTTING GUIDE FOR ART DECO BLOCKS

1 Cut the fabrics for the Art Deco blocks, following the cutting diagrams for each piece.

DARK SILK FABRICS

Asterisk (*) indicates pieces are interfaced.

Fabric	Pattern	Description	Quantity
#1 Russet dupioni	Binding	33" x 1¾" on straight of grain	Cut 1 length
Backing	Middle strip	7" x 44" piece	Cut 1
	A	*Curved diamond Center	Cut 1
	B	*Quarter circle	Cut 4
	C	*Outer ring	Cut 2 one half pieces
	D	*Small diamond center	Cut 1
	X	*5 ½" square	Cut 1

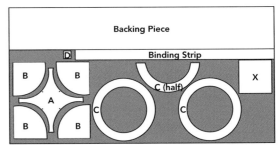

Fabric #1 Russet dupioni cutting diagram.

Fabric	Pattern	Description	Quantity
#2 Brown geometric print	A	*Curved diamond center	Cut 1
	B	*Quarter circle	Cut 4
	C	*Outer ring	Cut 1
	D	*Small diamond center	Cut 1

Fabric #2 Brown geometric print cutting diagram.

Fabric	Pattern	Description	Quantity
#3 Black geometric print	A	*Curved diamond center	Cut 2 one half pieces
	B	*Quarter circle	Cut 4
	C	*Outer ring	Cut 1
	D	*Small diamond center	Cut 1
	X	*5 ½" square	Cut 1

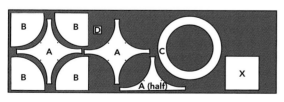

Fabric #3 Black geometric print cutting diagram.

Fabric	Pattern	Description	Quantity
#4 Brown Shadow dupioni	Binding	33" x 1¾" on straight of grain	Cut 1 length
	A	*Curved diamond center	Cut 1
	B	*Quarter circle	Cut 4
	C	*Outer ring	Cut 1
	D	*Small diamond center	Cut 1

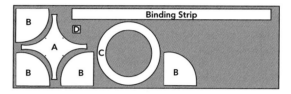

Fabric #4 Brown Shadow dupioni cutting diagram.

LIGHT SILK FABRICS

Fabric	Pattern	Description	Quantity
#5 Cream/ tan waves print	A	*Curved diamond center	Cut 2
	B	*Quarter circle	Cut 11
	C	*Outer ring	Cut none
	D	*Small diamond center	Cut 1

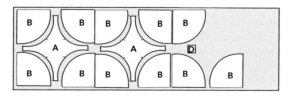

Fabric #5 Cream with tan wave print cutting diagram.

Fabric	Pattern	Description	Quantity
#6 Fawn dupioni	Backing (top strip)	36" x 44" piece	Cut 1
	A	Curved diamond center	Cut none
	B	*Quarter circle	Cut 2
	C	*Outer ring	Cut 2
	D	*Small diamond center	Cut 2
	G (for Lady)	1920s Lady's hand (appliqué)	Cut 1 with allowance
	H (for Lady)	1920s Lady's Face (appliqué)	Cut 1 with allowance

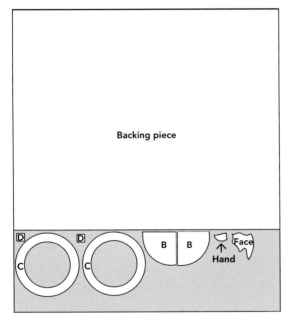

Fabric #6 Fawn dupioni, cutting diagram. Refer to Pattern Notes (on page 51) when cutting the 1920s Lady's Hand and Face.

Fabric	Pattern	Description	Quantity
#7 Lavender blush dupioni	Backing (bottom strip)	24" x 44" piece	Cut 1
	A	*Curved diamond center	Cut none
	B	*Quarter circle	Cut 5
	C	*Outer ring	Cut 1
	D	*Small diamond center	Cut 2

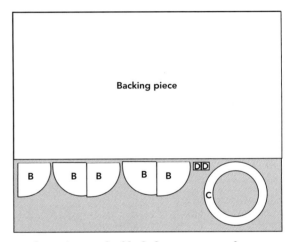

Fabric #7 Lavender blush dupioni cutting diagram.

Fabric	Pattern	Description	Quantity
#8 Lt. maize dupioni	A	*Curved diamond center	Cut two
	B	*Quarter circle	Cut 4
	C	*Outer ring	Cut 1
	D	*Small diamond center	Cut none

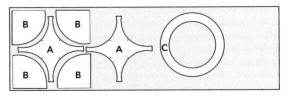

Fabric #8 Maize dupioni.

DUMMY BLOCKS

Fabric	Pattern	Description	Quantity
Muslin	X	5½" x 5½"	Cut 2
	Y	5½" x 10½"	Cut 3
	Z	10½" x 10½"	Cut 3

CUTTING GUIDE FOR ART NOUVEAU FLOURISHES

Pattern notes: The paper patterns included in this book are sturdy enough to be used for pressing to create a finished edge for appliqué, in the same manner as would freezer paper patterns. With this in mind, the paper patterns serve two purposes: to use as a cutting pattern and to use as an edge for pressing. For the Art Nouveau flourishes and Lady, dotted edges on patterns indicate those edges are to be prepared for appliqué. Edges without any markings indicate a ¼" underlap allowance. Edges with dashed lines indicate an outer edge with ⅜" seam allowance added. Cut out paper patterns very cleanly along dotted edges so that pattern can be adequately used for appliqué prep process.

2 Cut the fabrics for the Art Nouveau flourishes, following the cutting diagrams for each piece and making certain to add the ¼" hand-drawn appliqué allowance along all dotted edges.

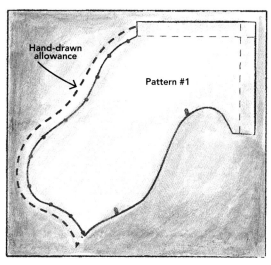

For appliqué patterns, a dotted edge indicates edge will be appliquéd. Hand draw an additional ¼" appliqué allowance on fabric along appliqué edge. You will cut fabric on the hand drawn edges.

FLOURISHES

Asterisk (°) indicates pieces are interfaced.

Fabric	Pattern	Description	Quantity
AA Dusty Purple Jacquard	1, 9, 14	°Applique	Cut 1 each
	Binding	33" x 1¾" on straight of grain	Cut 1 length

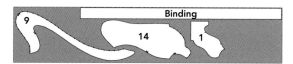

Fabric AA Dusty Purple Jacquard cutting diagram.

Fabric	Pattern	Description	Quantity
BB Dusty lavender brocade	8, 16, 21	*Appliqué	Cut 1 each
	Binding	33" x 1¾" on straight of grain	Cut 1 length
	Rod pocket	5" x 26"	Cut 1 piece

Binding

Rod pocket

8

21

16

Fabric BB Dusty lavender Brocade cutting diagram.

Fabric	Pattern	Description	Quantity
CC Orange/rust Chiffon Burnout	7, 15, 22	*Appliqué (use black interfacing)	Cut 1 each

7 15 22

Fabric CC Orange/Rust Chiffon Burnout cutting diagram. Use black interfacing for this piece.

Fabric	Pattern	Description	Quantity
DD Burgundy brocade	6, 11, 19	*Appliqué	Cut 1 each

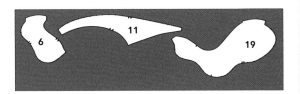

6 11 19

Fabric DD Burgundy Brocade cutting diagram.

Fabric	Pattern	Description	Quantity
EE Plum dupioni	5, 18	Appliqué	Cut 1 each

18 5

Fabric EE Plum dupioni, cutting diagram.

Fabric	Pattern	Description	Quantity
FF Dusty burgundy Jacquard	3, 17, 20	*Appliqué	Cut 1 each
	Binding	33" x 1¾" on straight of grain	Cut 1 length

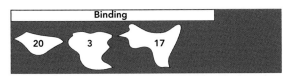

Binding

20 3 17

Fabric FF Dusty burgundy jacquard cutting diagram.

Fabric	Pattern	Description	Quantity
GG Heliotrope linen-weave/ slubs	2, 12, 13	*Appliqué	Cut 1 each

2 13 12

Fabric GG Heliotrope linen-weave with slubs cutting diagram.

Fabric	Pattern	Description	Quantity
HH Pistachio dupioni	4, 10	*Appliqué	Cut 1 each

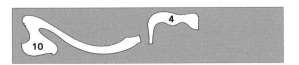

4 10

Fabric HH Pistachio dupioni cutting diagram.

MACHINE EMBROIDER THE LADY'S GARMENT SILK

3 Before cutting out the parts for the 1920s Lady, apply fusible knit interfacing to the entire piece of coffee bean dupioni on the backside. Now, machine embroider the silk piece. I used a leaf motif set at one repeat. The embroidery was scattered somewhat randomly with spaces of about 3" between individual motifs.

Embroidery notes: Test the motif you'd like to use on scrap fabric. Determine size, spacing and thread color when testing. Remember that the lady is in silhouette, so the embroidery should remain very subtle. After testing a few color choices, I decided upon black for the top embroidery thread and dusty purple for the bobbin thread. I also used paper backing on the fabric, as it was easy to tear away.

CUTTING GUIDE FOR 1920S LADY

4 Cut the fabrics for the Lady, following the cutting diagram and making certain to add the ¼" hand-drawn appliqué allowance along all dotted edges. Please note that cutting diagram for the Lady's face and hand is shown at Step 1, for fabric #6 Fawn dupioni.

Fabric	Pattern	Description	Quantity
#9 Coffee bean dupioni	Left shoe A	Appliqué	Cut 1
	Right shoe B	Appliqué	Cut 1
	Skirt C	Appliqué (has stitching details)	Cut 1
	Bustle D	Appliqué (has stitching details)	Cut 1
	Bodice E	Appliqué	Cut 1
	Sleeve F	Appliqué (has stitching details)	Cut 1
	Hair I	Appliqué	Cut 1
	Hat J	Appliqué	Cut 1

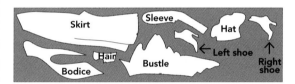

Fabric #9 coffee bean dupioni cutting diagram.

ASSEMBLE ART DECO BLOCKS

Construction notes: The Art Deco block section has fifteen blocks altogether, nine and one-half that are Art Deco blocks and five and one-half that are dummy blocks. Those dummy blocks act as a foundation upon which the flourishes can be built. You will notice that block #3 is half of an Art Deco block and about half of block #13 will be trimmed away eventually.

5 Following the Fabric Key below, place together Curved Diamond Center fabric elements (Art Deco blocks pattern A) with corresponding quarter Circle fabric elements (Art Deco blocks pattern B) for Art Deco blocks #1, 2, 4, 5, 7, 8, 10, 11 and 13. Place together the fabric elements needed for dummy blocks #3, 6, 9, 12, 14 and 15. Follow the diagram below to help you with this task.

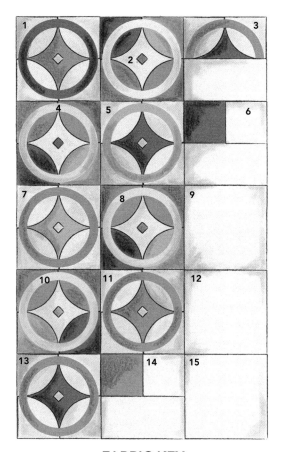

FABRIC KEY

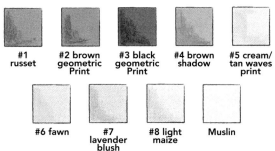

| #1 russet | #2 brown geometric Print | #3 black geometric Print | #4 brown shadow | #5 cream/tan waves print |

| #6 fawn | #7 lavender blush | #8 light maize | Muslin |

Assembly diagram for Art Deco and dummy blocks.

6 Working with the elements for block #1, sew a quarter circle to one edge of the curved diamond center, using ¼" seam allowance. Work with the curved diamond center on top, making certain to match the center marks of curved diamond center and quarter circle. Clip edge of curved diamond center close to but not through seam allowance before sewing.

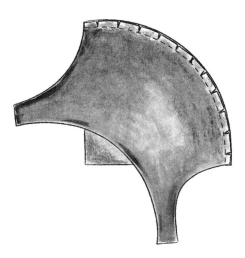

Sew one edge of the curved diamond center to one quarter circle, matching center marks and clipping the curved diamond center close to seam allowance.

Press seam allowance toward the curved diamond center. Continue to sew the other quarter circles to the remaining curved diamond center edges in the same manner, completing the assembly of block #1.

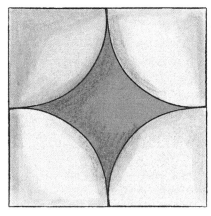

Assembled Art Deco block #1.

7 Assemble the remaining Art Deco blocks #'s 2, 4, 5, 7, 8, 10, 11 and 13, following the step 6 instructions.

8 Assemble the upper half of block #3, then complete it with one of the 5½" x 10½" muslin pieces.

9 Assemble the remaining dummy blocks, following assembly diagram for Art Deco and Dummy Blocks.

10 Measure the blocks. They should each be a 10½" square. Trim the blocks ever-so-slightly if necessary to be square. It is possible to fudge the seams a bit when sewing, so keep this in mind.

11 Sew the 15 blocks together in horizontal rows, following the numerical order shown in the assembly diagram on opposite page. Press seam allowances open.

Construction notes: You may prefer to press seam allowances to one side. When sewing interfaced silks, I always press seam allowances of this nature open.

OUTER RINGS

Construction notes: The outer rings are prepped as for appliqué and overlaid onto the pieced blocks. I found this to be the most successful and least frustrating assembly method.

Appliqué notes: Preparing the inner edge of the outer rings for appliqué can be somewhat tricky. Making an appliqué pattern from quilter's freezer paper is helpful. When the shiny side of the paper is pressed onto the interfaced side of the silk, the paper adheres and prepping the inner edge becomes easier.

12 Prep outer rings for appliqué. Place Outer Ring Appliqué Pattern , wrong-side up, on #3 outer ring fabric piece, interfaced-side up. Using a steam iron, press outer raw edge of fabric up and over onto paper pattern, shaping the outer edge into a perfect circle.

Clip the inward curves, then press inner raw edge up and over onto paper pattern. When pressing, be careful to not form points along inner or outer edges. Use a bit of water spray if necessary to achieve a crisp edge. Remove paper pattern. Press fabric edges again from both the interfaced and right sides. Repeat for each outer ring.

13 Pin outer rings in place on pieced Art Deco blocks, following fabric key on assembly diagram, page 54. Machine appliqué the rings in place, using a very small blind hem stitch and neutral thread. Test stitch size on scrap fabric. The outer rings are ⅛" smaller all around than finished block size.

14 Press the outer edges of each small diamond center under ¼". Pin small diamond centers to center of blocks #1, 2, 4, 5, 7, 8, 10, 11 and 13. Machine or hand sew in place.

ASSEMBLE ART
NOUVEAU FLOURISHES

15 Prep the flourishes for appliqué. Beginning with flourish pattern #1, place pattern, wrong-side up, on #1 flourish fabric piece, interfaced side up. Press appliqué edge (dotted edge on pattern) of fabric up and over onto paper pattern. Clip inward *but not* outward curves before pressing. Pin prepped piece to assembled Art Deco blocks at the upper right corner.

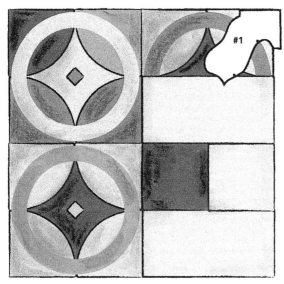

Flourish piece #1 is pinned to the upper right corner of the assembled Art Deco blocks.

16 Continue to prep each flourish piece, working in numerical order. After each piece is prepped, pin it in place on the Art Deco blocks piece, as shown in the diagram below.

FABRIC KEY

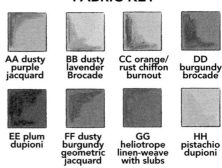

| AA dusty purple jacquard | BB dusty lavender Brocade | CC orange/ rust chiffon burnout | DD burgundy brocade |

| EE plum dupioni | FF dusty burgundy geometric jacquard | GG heliotrope linen-weave with slubs | HH pistachio dupioni |

Pin each prepared flourish piece in place on the Art Deco blocks piece, working in numerical order as much as possible.

17 Hand or machine sew the flourish pieces in place.

ASSEMBLE 1920S LADY

18 Prep the 1920s Lady pieces for appliqué. The more careful and precise you are with pressing the edges to the wrong side, the more detailed the Lady will appear. As before, clip all inward *not* outward curves before pressing and press well from wrong and right fabric sides once paper pattern has been removed.

19 Several of the Lady's garment pieces are detailed with stitching, which include skirt C, bustle D and sleeve F. Using light gold machine embroidery thread, stitch the garment detail lines on the skirt C and bustle D. A double straight stitch works great for this task. Do not sew the sleeve detailing just yet.

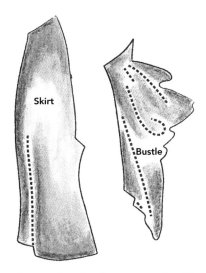

Machine embroider the garment detail lines, using a double straight stitch.

20 For hat J, cut two 5" lengths from the dusty purple grosgrain ribbon. Tack one end from each length to the back of the piece near the brim" area. Turn piece over. Tie ribbons as for a very loose knot and extend ends to opposite sides, then around to the back of the piece. Tack ends in place on Hat back. Tack ribbon at center front too.

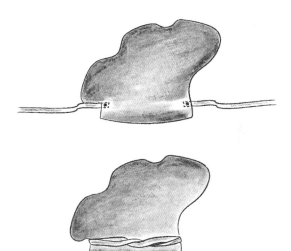

Tie grosgrain ribbon around hat brim very loosely.

21 Pin the Lady together, following the diagram below, but do not pin her to the quilt, although you might want to place the Lady on the quilt to make sure she has the right stance. When pleased with her form, hand sew the elements together where they overlap. Machine embroider Sleeve F garment detail lines, as with step 20.

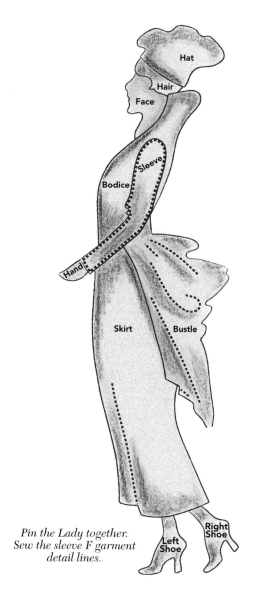

Pin the Lady together. Sew the sleeve F garment detail lines.

22 Pin the Lady to the quilt and hand or machine sew her in place along all outer edges. The Lady covers some outer flourish edges.

MAKING THE BACKING

23 Press the russet, fawn and lavender blush backing pieces. Sew the russet piece to the fawn piece along one 44" edge, right sides facing, using a ½" seam allowance. Sew the lavender blush piece to the russet piece along the remaining 44" edge, right sides facing, using a ½" seam allowance. Press seam allowances open.

24 Use masking tape to temporarily secure backing to work surface, wrong-side up. Lightly press a piece of batting, but only if it is a natural fiber, as suggested in the materials list. Center batting over backing. Center quilt over batting/backing. Pin and baste stitch the three layers together, using your favorite method. I prefer to baste with thread. Remove masking tape.

FREE-MOTION QUILT THE QUILT

25 Beginning with the Lady, free-motion quilt her garment. Free-motion quilt hand and face, using the black embroidery thread and a meandering approach, or your own personal style. Free-motion quilt the Art Deco blocks, following the pattern of the blocks and using somewhat matching threads. Free-motion quilt the flourishes, following the lines of the flourishes a bit and using somewhat matching threads.

26 Trim the left edge of the quilt as shown in the diagram below. Trim away the excess muslin at bottom right corner as well. Mark cutting line with pins to help with trimming decision.

The left edge of the quilt is trimmed with a curved shape before being finished with binding.

BIND THE QUILT

27 Trim ends of each binding strip with a 45-degree angle. Sew strips together along diagonal edges, keeping brown tones on one end and plum tones on other end. Press seam allowances open. Press binding in half, matching long edges.

28 Sew binding to outer edge of quilt, right sides facing, using a scant ¼" seam allowance. Sew again ⅛" to the right of first row of stitching. Trim excess quilt and binding away close to second row of stitching. Wrap binding snugly around to backside of quilt so that the amount of binding showing on quilt front is no wider than ¼". Hand sew edge of binding to back of quilt.

Sew Binding to quilt outer edge using a ¼" seam allowance.

MAKE THE ROD POCKET

29 Sew ½" double hems on both short edges of rod pocket piece. Press. Sew one long rod pocket edge to top edge of quilt, right sides facing, using a ¼" seam allowance. Sew again ⅛" to the right of first row of stitching. Trim excess and overcast seam allowance. Press rod pocket strip upward. Overcast remaining rod pocket long edge. Press overcast edge under ¼". Fold rod pocket to backside of quilt and pin pressed edge over sewn top edge. Hand sew rod pocket in place.

MAKE THE BOUQUET

30 Make a small ribbon work flower bouquet for the Lady to hold. Follow the illustrations to make the flowers.

Ribbon	Technique	Cut length	Quantity
Dark lavender cross-dyed	Rosebud	5"	2
	Rose with half ruffle	7"	1

1. Fold right end forward, diagonally.

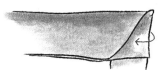

2. Fold right end over.

3. Roll end forward. Tack roll ¼" up from lower edge, forming center.

4. Fold ribbon to the back diagonally.

5. Wrap fold around upper edge of center, tacking ribbon in place at lower edge. Fold again.

6. Finished rosebud.

7. For rose with half-ruffle, sew gathered ribbon around rosebud.

8. Finished rose with half ruffle.

Ribbonwork rosebud and rose with half ruffle technique.

Ribbon	Technique	Cut length	Quantity
Lavender ombré	Ruffled petal	5"	1
Orange bias cut	Ruffled petal	5"	1
Dusty purple bias cut	Ruffled petal	2½"	3

1. Gather stitch length of ribbon as shown. Pull thread to gather ribbon. Knot thread.

2. Finished Ruffled petal.

Ribbonwork ruffled petal technique.

Ribbon	Technique	Cut length	Quantity
Dusty purple grosgrain	Folded leaf	1½"	3

1. Fold ribbon end diagonally forward.

2. Fold other end diagonally forward. Gather stitch, pull thread to gather ribbon. Knot thread.

3. Finished Folded leaf.

Ribbonwork folded leaf technique.

31 Sew the ribbonwork pieces to a base of wool felt, crisp interfacing or crinoline. Trim away excess base. Hand sew base to lady's hand. Tie small bow with 7mm silk ribbon. Sew knot of bow just below ribbonwork cluster. Tie knots in ribbon ends and cut ends at a slant.

ADD THE BEADS

32 Sew ten 3mm round beads to outer edge of Lady's bodice, beginning near waist about ½" upward from sleeve. Space beads so they are 1" apart. Sew two 3mm round beads to each shoe instep outer edge, spacing beads about ¼" apart.

33 Sew sequins to Art Deco blocks at cross points, anchoring each sequin with a small seed bead.

34 Sew three long bead dangles to the bottom right edge of the quilt. The outermost dangle is about 3½" long. The middle dangle is about 4½" long and the inner dangle is about 5½" long. Refer to general instructions on page 9 for making a bead dangle.

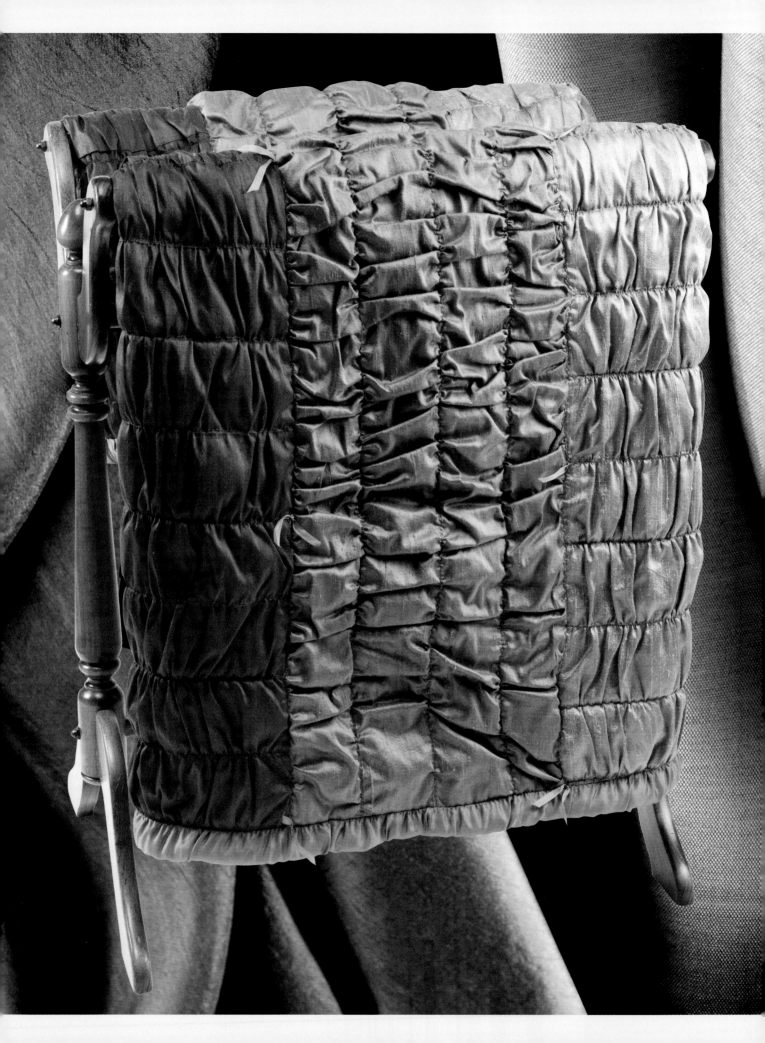

Gathering Warmth

THE SHIRRED TEXTURE CREATED for this modern, yet cozy blanket is yummy. The silk habutai fabric that is the backing and binding, combines softly with the wool batting for a blanket that is lighter than air.

MATERIALS

Silk fabrics:
   1⅞ yd. Copper silk dupioni

   1½ yd. Patina silk dupioni

   1⅛ yd. Sand silk dupioni

   3⅝ yd. Café silk habutai (for backing and binding)

Other supplies and tools:
   66" x 66" piece of wool batting

7 yd. of 7mm Gold silk ribbon

One ball of Ivory 30-weight cotton crochet thread

Size 20 chenille needle

Sewing thread: matching for each piece of silk and a neutral shade

Iron and ironing board

Sewing machine plus basic accessories

For shirring: buttonhole foot with center toe, gathering stitch

Basic sewing supplies

Finished size: about 60" x 60"

Construction notes: To easily accomplish the shirring, four things are needed: A buttonhole foot with center front toe, 30-weight cotton crochet thread, the gathering stitch on your sewing machine and thread to match each shade of silk.

CUTTING GUIDE

Cut the fabrics as shown in the chart below.

Fabric	Description	Cut size and amount
Patina dupioni	Horizontal-shirred Bands A and C	Cut 4 13" x 44" strips
Copper dupioni	Vertically-shirred Band B	Cut 1 19" x 44" strip
		One 19" x 18" piece
	Horizontally-shirred Band E	Cut 2 strips 13" x 44" strips
Sand dupioni	Vertically-shirred Band D	Cut 1 strip 19" x 44"
		1 piece 19" x 18"
Café habutai	Backing	Cut 1 length 64" x 44"
		2 lengths 64" x 10"
	Binding	Cut 6 strips 60" x 4"

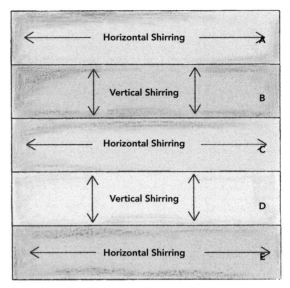

Diagram of blanket showing horizontal and vertical rows.

PIECE THE BANDS

½" seam allowance unless otherwise noted.

1 For Bands A and C, sew two Patina 13" strips together along one 13" edge for each band, right sides facing. For band E, sew two copper 13" strips together along one 13" edge, right sides facing. For band B, sew the copper 19" x 44" strip to the 19" x 18" piece along one 19" edge, right sides facing. For band D, sew the sand 19" x 44" strip to the 19" x 18" piece along one 19" edge, right sides facing. Press seam allowances open.

SHIRRING THE BANDS

Construction notes: To mark the bands for shirring, a pressing technique is used. Bands are folded and pressed in half, either vertically or horizontally. Then, at 3" intervals from the center, bands are pressed again until each band is thoroughly marked for shirring. For the horizontally-shirred bands (A, C, E), there will be three pressed shirring marks. For the vertically-shirred bands (B, D), there will be eighteen pressed shirring marks.

2 Mark bands A, C and E for horizontal rows of shirring by pressing at center and 3" intervals from center. Mark bands B and D for vertical rows of shirring by pressing.

3 Beginning with band A, sew shirring rows along each pressed mark and at the seam allowances. Here's how:

Place Band A on sewing table, wrong-side up.

Cut a length of 30-weight cotton crochet thread a bit longer than twice as long as band (band is about 88" long, so thread cut length should be about 174").

Fold thread in half. Hook the center loop over the center toe on the buttonhole foot and take both thread ends toward the back of the machine.

Use the gathering stitch with a width of 4.2mm and depth of 1.0mm.

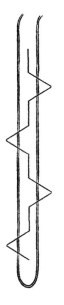

Sew gathering stitch over 30-weight thread on wrong side of fabric.

Sew over 30-weight thread with the gathering stitch along the length of band A's pressed center mark, using thread to match fabric. Trim sewing thread, but not 30-weight cotton thread. You may wish to practice this technique.

Continue sewing lengths of the 30-weight thread over each pressed mark, working with fabric wrong side up. Sew the shirring rows along edges at the seam line as well.

Pull both 30-weight threads from center, shirring fabric, until shirred length measures 60". Tie a set of 30-weight threads together three times at end from which the threads have been pulled. Trim away excess thread, leaving 5" ends to safeguard against thread knot unraveling. Repeat with each set of threads.

Continue to pull the 30-weight threads, working one shirred row at a time, measuring gathered rows to size and knotting threads each time.

4 Work band B with the same shirring technique as with step 4, sewing vertical rows. Since the fabric width is 19", the length of the 30-weight thread should be about 45" for each shirred row. When pulling threads, gather fabric down to 13" in width and secure 30-weight thread.

5 Sew shirring rows for the remaining bands C, D and E, following steps 4 and 5.

SEW THE BANDS TOGETHER

6 Evenly adjust the gathers on each band. Sew the bands together in alphabetical order, right sides facing.

QUILT THE BLANKET

7 Place batting on work surface. Center blanket over batting, right side up. Pin layers together.

8 Machine sew blanket to batting along shirred rows and seam lines, using the serpentine stitch and the neutral thread shade. Set stitch width at 1.2 and stitch depth at .08.

BACK AND BIND THE BLANKET

9 Sew the two 10" backing pieces to either side of the 44" -wide backing piece along 64" long edges, right sides facing. Press seam allowances open.

10 Place backing on work surface, wrong side up. Center quilted blanket on backing, right side up. Pin layers together

11 Sew the binding strips together along the 4" edges, right sides facing and sew first strip to last. Press seam allowances open. Press one long edge under ½". The pressed-under edge will be wrapped to the blanket back. Sew shirring rows along the pressed-under edge and the opposite edge (this edge will be sewn to the blanket front), sewing the shirring rows for a space of one strip's worth for manage-ability and using the same shirring technique as with step 4 on opposite page.

12 Pull shirring threads to gather binding. Adjust shirring so that gathered Binding measures about 240". Pin binding edge with seam allowance to blanket front, right sides facing, adjusting gathers as necessary. Sew binding to blanket through all layers. Trim excess batting with a 1¼" allowance past seam line.

13 Wrap binding around to backside of blanket. Pull shirring threads to gather pressed-under binding edge. Adjust gathers and pin edge in place on backside of blanket, enclosing bat-ting and binding scam allowance. Hand sew in place, making certain to first knot shirring threads. Trim excess thread away.

TIE THE BLANKET AND BACKING TOGETHER

14 Cut 36 pieces 7" long from 7mm silk ribbon. Use a chenille needle to sew ribbon through blanket front, batting, backing, and back up to front. Tie ends together two times. Trim ribbons a bit.

A Poet's Garden

A QUILT IS A PIECE OF ART, no doubt inspired by a restless dream or a moment of quietness. A canvas frame seems to be the perfect form on which to wrap a quilted reverie, an art quilt in which color and texture swirl together. The Echinacea flower image that has been recreated in A Poet's Garden had just the right amount of subtle movement that I was looking for to express the powerful calm of nature that begs us to listen.

MATERIALS

Note: Refer to Fabric Key on page 81

Silk fabrics:

1 yd. 44"-wide light pink silk dupioni (backdrop, lettering)

1 piece silk dupioni 7½" x 10½" for each of the following shades: Poppy, beauty, raspberry, terra cotta, persimmon, tangerine, pumpkin, russet, brown shadow (petals)

1 piece each 14" x 18" new fern and avocado skin silk dupioni (leaf and stems)

6½" x 6½" Shadow silk dupioni (flower center)

5" x 22" Cameo silk dupioni (lettering)

1⅝" x 44" strip each bullion and sunset gold silk dupioni (flower center ruffle)

5½" x 8½" piece paper-mounted silk chiffon for inkjet printing the letter N. You can substitute with any other paper-mounted silk or cotton, if preferred

Embellishments:

2 yd. of ⅛"-diameter satin cording (to gather stems)

Assorted mixture of iridescent white, pink and crystal beads and sequins (about 20–30 beads and sequins altogether)

Other supplies and tools:

1 yd. 44"-wide muslin (backing)

2½ yd. 20"-wide lightweight, fusible knit interfacing

5½" x 5½" fusible fleece or needle punch batting (flower center)

32" x 38" silk, wool or cotton batting

24" x 30" canvas frame with 1½" side edges

6½" x 6½" piece of quilter's freezer paper

Iron and ironing board

Sewing machine with basic accessories and darning foot for free-motion quilting

Basic sewing supplies

Self-healing cutting mat

Rotary cutter

Grid lined ruler

Scissors, fabric and craft

Sewing threads: Neutral and matching

Large-eyed bodkin

Pencil

Masking tape

Four color inkjet printer

Desktop publishing software

Staple gun

A Poet's Garden patterns: Petals A, B, C, D, E, F, G, H, I, J, K, L, M, N, O, P, Q, R, S, T, U, V, W, X, U. Flower center Z. Left side of Leaf. Right side of Leaf. Letters L, I, S, T, E, N.

Finished size: 24" x 30"

Brief overview of the steps for making A Poet's Garden: Once fabrics are cut, petals, leaf and letters are prepared for appliqué. Stems must also be sewn and readied. Next, the backdrop is prepared with batting and backing. Before letters, leaf and petals are appliquéd in place, stems are sewn to the layered backdrop and the upper right and lower left portions of the backdrop are free-motion quilted. The piece is finished with the flower center and bits of beading.

CUTTING FABRICS

Pattern notes: The paper patterns included in this book are sturdy enough to be used for pressing to create a finished edge for appliqué, in the same manner as would freezer paper patterns. With this in mind, the paper patterns serve two purposes: to use as a cutting pattern and to use as an edge for pressing. Dotted edges on patterns indicate those edges are to be prepared for appliqué. Edges with a dashed line indicate ¼" seam allowance or underlap allowance. Cut out paper patterns very cleanly along dotted edges so that pattern can be adequately used for appliqué prep process.

Cutting notes: The dotted edges of paper patterns do not have an appliqué allowance. Hand draw an additional ¼" appliqué allowance on fabric prior to cutting pieces out. You will cut fabric on the hand drawn edges.

Cutting fabrics notes: Dotted edges indicate appliqué edge. Dashed edge indicates underlap allowance.

CUTTING GUIDE

Fabric	Pattern	Description	Quantity
Fusible fleece	Z	Cut ⅛" smaller all around than pattern	1 piece
Silks:			
Poppy dupioni	A, H, P, V	Petals. Appliqué process	1 each
Beauty dupioni	B, I, O, W	Petals. Appliqué process	1 each
Raspberry dupioni	C, J, Q, Y	Petals. Appliqué process	1 each
Terra Cotta dupioni	D, K, S	Petals. Appliqué process	1 each
Persimmon dupioni	E, L, R, U	Petals. Appliqué process	1 each
Tangerine dupioni	F, M, T	Petals. Appliqué process	1 each
Pumpkin dupioni	G, N, X	Petals. Appliqué process	1 each
Russet dupioni	A, D, R	Petal shadows. Appliqué process	1 each
Brown shadow dupioni.	F, I, L	Petal shadows. Appliqué process	1 each
Shadow dupioni	Z	Flower center. Appliqué process	1 piece
New fern dupioni	Leaf (left-side)	Appliqué process	1 piece
	Stems	1⅛" bias strips	About 60"
Avocado Skin dup.	Leaf (right-side)	Appliqué process	1 piece
	Stems	1⅛" bias strips	About 30"
Lt. Pink dupioni	Backdrop	33" x 39"	1 piece
	Lettering	5" x 22". Do not be concerned with grainline	1 piece

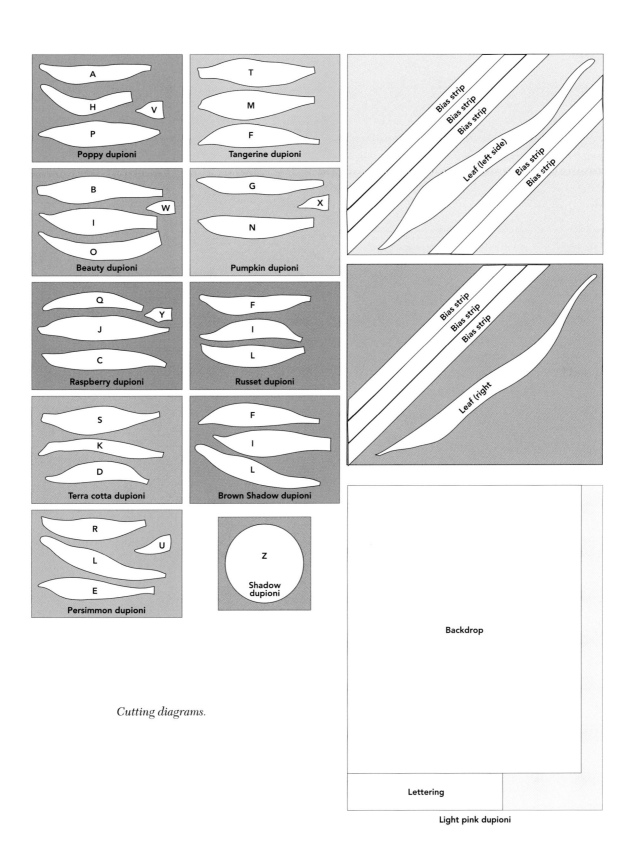

Cutting diagrams.

1 Cut the following from lightweight, fusible knit interfacing: For Petals, cut nine 7½" x 10½" pieces. For Flower Center, cut one 6½" x 6½" piece. For Lettering, cut two 5" x 22" pieces. From smooth side (side without adhesive) of interfacing, cut one left side and one right side of Leaf, placing Leaf patterns wrong side up on interfacing when cutting.

2 Apply 7½" x 10½" interfacing pieces to backsides of poppy, beauty, raspberry, terra cotta, persimmon, tangerine, pumpkin, russet and brown shadow dupioni pieces.
*Refer to the fabric key diagram on page 81.
Note: Petal Patterns have been grouped together according to fabric shade on the pull-out pattern sheet. Match pattern petal groups with appropriate fabric before beginning to cut. Regroup petals for "shadow" fabrics.

3 Working with the poppy piece, place A, H, P and V paper patterns, wrong side up, onto interfaced side of fabric. Hand draw a ¼" appliqué allowance onto fabric along dotted edges indicated on patterns, using a pencil. Cut out Petals from fabric

4 Referring to Cutting Guide, continue to cut all Petals from interfaced pieces of silk.

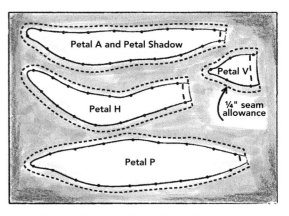

Step 3: Cut Petals from fabric along the ¼" hand-drawn seam allowance. Keep in mind that the narrow, straight edge has a ¼" underlap allowance included on pattern.

5 Apply 5" x 22" fusible knit interfacing pieces to backside of light pink and cameo dupioni pieces.

6 Sew the 5" x 22" cameo and light pink silk pieces together, right sides facing, along one 22" edge, using a ¼" seam allowance. Press seam allowance open. Place L, I, S, T, E and N backwards onto interfaced side of seamed fabric. Hand draw a ¼" appliqué allowance along all edges, using a pencil. Cut out letters from fabric.

Step 8: With letters placed backwards onto wrong side of seamed piece, add the ¼" appliqué allowance all around each letter. Cut out letters along hand-drawn lines.

PREPARE PETALS, LEAF AND LETTERING FOR APPLIQUÉ

7 Place Petal A paper pattern, wrong side up, onto Petal A fabric piece, interface-side up. Using a steam iron, press raw edge of fabric up and over onto paper pattern, shaping a perfect petal. Clip all inward curves, *not* outward curves. When pressing, be careful to not form points along edges. Use a bit of water spray if necessary to achieve a crisp edge. Remove paper pattern. Press fabric petal edges again from both the interfaced and right sides. Repeat for each petal. Keep in mind that the russet and brown shadow silk petals A, D, F, I, L and R are petal shadows. Set prepared petals aside for now. You may find it helpful to keep the petals in alphabetical order.

Step 9: Prepare each petal piece for appliqué by pressing fabric raw edge up and over onto paper pattern.

8 Place left side of Leaf paper pattern, wrong side up, onto left side of Leaf fabric piece, interfaced side up. Prepare for appliqué as with petals in step 9. Remember that the entire right edge of the left-side of the Leaf is an underlap edge. Repeat this process for the right side of the Leaf. The right side does not have underlap edges, except at the bottom-most tip. Set leaf pieces aside.

9 Place the letter L paper pattern, wrong side up, onto interface-side of the letter L fabric piece. Prepare for appliqué as with petals in step 9. Be careful to achieve a clean finished edge so that lettering is quite crisp in appearance. Inward corners are the most difficult to prepare, so just be patient with yourself. Repeat for each letter. Once appliquéd, those inward corner trouble spots disappear. Set letters aside.

PRINT THE SPECIAL
IMAGE FOR LETTER N

With regard to the silk chiffon, you have several alternatives with the printing images step: you can purchase silk chiffon that already is paper-backed, scan and print the image from your home computer and inkjet printer, using a desktop publishing program, or design your own image and print onto the silk chiffon. The directions below assume you will need to prepare the chiffon for printing.

10 Scan image "A Poet's Garden" on page 123 and place into a 5½" x 8½" sized file, making sure to enlarge image 200%. Place piece of paper-backed silk chiffon into your printer with the appropriate side up for your printer. Print special image for letter N onto the chiffon, making certain to change paper size to 5½" x 8½" before printing. Let ink dry. Peel away paper backing and cut out letter N from chiffon along dashed line (appliqué allowance has been added).

11 Trace letter N pattern, wrong side up, onto mat size of freezer paper. Cut out letter. Press freezer paper N onto wrong side of chiffon. Prepare piece for appliqué as with all other letters. Set chiffon letter aside for now.

PREPARE STEMS

12 Machine sew the 1⅛"-wide new fern and avocado skin bias cuts together, using a ¼" seam allowance and sewing the two different strip shades together randomly and forming one long Stem strip. Make certain the ends of each individual strip are diagonally cut before sewing them together. Press seam allowances open.

Step 14: Sew bias strip ends together along diagonal edges.

13 Press both long edges of the stem strip under ¼" to wrong side, then press in half, matching pressed-under edges. Sew together close to pressed-under edges, forming a long, flat Stem. Using a bodkin, slip satin cording through entire length of Stem channel, pinning cording end to channel entry point so as not to lose the end within the channel. Pull on cording from opposite end so that flat Stem gathers down to about 60". Set stems aside.

Step 15: Slip satin cording through Stem channel. The cording is used to easily gather Stems.

PREPARE BACKGROUND

14 Press muslin and light pink dupioni backdrop piece. Carefully press batting, but only if it is a natural fiber, as suggested in the materials list. Use masking tape to temporarily secure muslin to work surface. Center batting over muslin.

15 Fold light pink dupioni backdrop piece in half to find the vertical center. Mark a 15" line from the backdrop top along the vertical center with pins. Fold the flower center pattern Z into quarters to find pattern center. Align center of pattern with cross mark on backdrop. Lightly trace around pattern Z onto backdrop with pencil to indicate positioning for flower petals.

16 Center pink dupioni backdrop piece over batting and muslin. Pin and baste layers together, using your favorite method. I prefer to baste with thread and for this art quilt, the basting can be widely spaced. Remove masking tape.

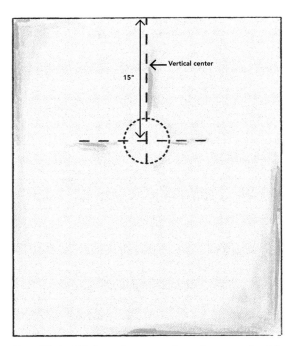

Step 17: At 15" down from top edge, place a mark with a pencil at vertical center of light pink backdrop piece. Center and trace pattern Z over mark.

SEW STEMS, LEAF AND
LETTER E IN PLACE

Assembly notes: In order to properly position stems and leaf, all other design elements must be temporarily placed onto backdrop. They will be removed before stems and leaf are sewn in place. Refer to the diagram on page 81.

19 Place Petals around traced circle, pinning them temporarily in place. Remember that the unfinished petal ends have a ¼" underlap allowance, so be certain those ends extend ¼" inward onto traced circle. Place lettering below the flower and temporarily pin in place. Place the leaf over the upper edge of the letter E and underneath petals G, F and E, also having the bottom left leaf edge against the right edge of petal H. Reposition elements as needed for a pleasing arrangement.

Step 19: The stems are strategically placed underneath petals, underneath the letters T and E, and near the leaf.

20 Beginning with the stem end underneath the left edge of the letter E, meander the stem underneath the letter T, up toward the bottom left edge of the leaf and right edge of the petal H, underneath the petals on the flower's right side and then over to upper left edge of the backdrop. The stem can be placed over rather than underneath these elements, as the elements will be removed shortly. Trim excess from stem at upper-left edge of backdrop, but be careful to secure cording within stem channel before trimming. Restart stem near petal T and meander as before, tucking end underneath the long stem at the starting point. It's okay for the stem to twist as it meanders.

21 When pleased with arrangement of the stems in conjunction with the petals, leaf and lettering, pin stems, leaf and the letter E in place. Be certain to tuck bottom tip of the leaf underneath the stem. Also, at the upper tip of the Leaf, it may be necessary to trim away some of the underlap allowance. Remove all petals and letters L, I, S, T and N.

22 Hand sew the stems in place along one edge. Machine sew letter E and leaf in place, using the blind hem-stitch and matching thread. Set stitch length to about 1.4mm and stitch width about 1.2mm. Test stitch size on a scrap fabric before sewing the actual leaf in place. The stitch should appear visually appealing and quite subtle. Reposition letter T and sew in place in the same manner.

FREE-MOTION QUILT THE BACKDROP

23 The upper-right corner of the backdrop is free-motion quilted between the smaller stem and upper edge of the leaf. The lower-right corner of the backdrop is free-motion quilted between the long stem and left edge of the letter T. Free-motion quilt these spaces, using a meandering approach, or your own personal style and a somewhat matching thread.

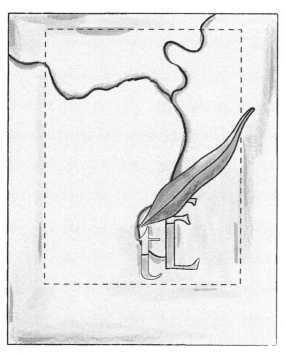

Step 22: The stems are hand-sewn in place. The letter E and the leaf are machine sewn in place, as is the letter T.

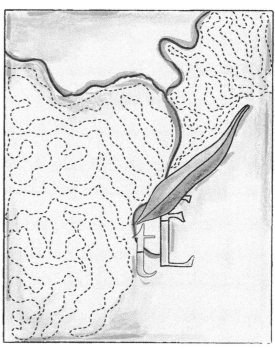

Step 23: Machine quilt upper-right and lower-left backdrop corners, using the free-motion quilting technique. Thread color can either be a perfect match to the backdrop or a close match.

SEW LETTERING AND PETALS IN PLACE

24 Reposition petals onto the backdrop in alphabetical order. Reposition and pin remaining letters, except for the chiffon N, onto backdrop. When pleased with the arrangement, sew all in place by machine, using somewhat matching threads and the same-sized blind hem stitch as in step 22.

25 Overlap chiffon N onto dupioni N, positioning it a scant ⅛" to the right and upward from the dupioni letter N. Machine sew in place, again using the blind hem stitch.

MAKE FLOWER CENTER

26 Place flower center Z paper pattern, wrong side up, onto flower center Z fabric piece, wrong side up. Prepare piece for appliqué as was done with step 9 for the petals. Do not clip outward curves. Press well. Apply fusible fleece circle to wrong side of flower center. If necessary, trim fleece a bit so that it will not show at all from right side of the flower center.

27 Press the 1⅝"-wide bullion and sunset gold strips. Cut one end on each piece at a 45-degree angle. Sew strips together along diagonal ends, using a ¼" seam allowance. Press seam allowances open. Press both long edges of strip under ¼", then press in half, matching pressed-under edges.

28 Machine gather-stitch along pressed-under edges. Pull thread ends so that the gathered strip measures about 55". Evenly adjust and direct gathers as much as possible. Pin gathered edge of strip close to outer edge of the flower center, tucking end underneath outer edge of the flower center. When the strip is near overlapping the beginning point, hand sew the gathered edge to the outer edge of flower center. Continue to pin the gathered edge of the strip to the flower center as it begins to swirl toward the middle. The swirling rows of the gathered strip should not overlap onto each other, allowing the rich Shadow shade to show through. Continue to hand sew a row at a time in place as it swirls toward the middle.

Step 28: Begin to pin gathered strip onto the outer edge of the flower center, hand-sewing the row in place before continuing to swirl strip toward the center.

29 Coil the gathered strip upon reaching the middle, trimming the excess strip away as needed. Hand sew in place.

30 Pin and hand sew the decorated piece to the center of the flower, hiding all raw petal edges.

BEAD UNQUILTED SPACES

31 Hand sew a random variety of beads and sequins onto unquilted portions of backdrop spaces. A very small quantity of beads is needed for this task. The slight amount of beads will occasionally catch the light.

MOUNT QUILT ONTO CANVAS FRAME

32 Place canvas frame on your work surface, right side up. Position and center the finished quilt over frame. The horizontal center of the flower should be about 10½" down from the top edge of the frame and the vertical center of the flower should be centered between the side edges of the frame. Once the quilt is properly placed, pin it to the canvas frame along all outer edges. If necessary, reposition the quilt to make certain you are pleased with the placement.

Step 32: Place the finished quilt over the frame, centered. Pin to the canvas along the outer edges.

33 Turn frame/quilt over to wrong side of frame. Working with the frame top, snugly wrap quilt excess around to frame back, at the center of the space. Fold raw edges under about 1½" so that turned-under edge will align with inner edge of frame on backside. It will probably be necessary for some of the excess fabric to be trimmed away to eliminate bulk. Staple fabric in place at center of frame top edge along the inner edge.

34 Now staple the quilt to the bottom inner edge of the frame at the center of the space. Staple quilt to side inner edges of frame at the center of the space. Continue to staple quilt to frame back, folding quilt edges under for a clean, finished edge, working small sections at a time. Pull quilt very taut with each motion and work opposite sides so that quilt will be evenly stretched around the frame. At corners, carefully trim away a small amount of bulk while folding the quilt fabric inward at the top and bottom corners. I found it helpful to pin the corners for this task. Fold excess carefully up onto frame back. Staple in place and remove all pins.

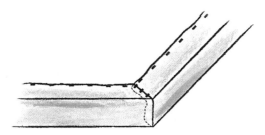

Step 34: Fold fabric very cleanly at outer corners when wrapping quilt around frame. Have folded edges be at the top and bottom corners, rather than being able to view the folded corners from side edges.

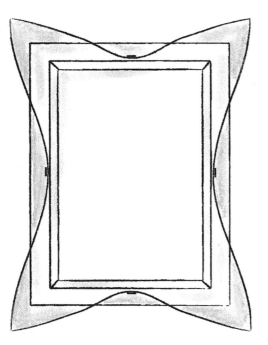

Step 33: Begin wrapping quilt around the frame along top, bottom and sides, stapling it in place at the inner center edges on the frame backside.

FABRIC KEY

#1 poppy #2 beauty #3 raspberry #4 terra cotta #5 persimmon #6 tangerine #7 pumpkin #8 russet

#9 brown shadow #10 new fern #11 avocado skin #12 light pink #13 cameo #14 shadow #15 bullion #16 sunset gold

A Poet's Garden diagram.

Wildly Charming

It's an elegant, period-style undergarment and it's a quilt. For my first book, I made a sweet, embellished vest that one of my daughter's claimed. We put it on display rather than it being hidden away in a closet. I love that vest and enjoy looking at the interesting work every day. One day my daughter will take it to her home and I'll miss it. This piece has been made so that it could be worn by a petite figure, but truly, it is a quilt. One of my most favorite fabrics, silk organza, graces this charming, quilted garment.

MATERIALS

Silk fabrics:
  ⅝ yd. of 44" light pink silk dupioni

  ½ yd. of blush silk dupioni

  ½ yd. of 54" light salmon silk shantung

  ½ yd. of 30"–36" blush silk metallic crinkle

  ⅓ yd. of 42"–54" off-white silk organza

  1 yd. of 44" cream with black dot silk crepe de chine

Embellishments:
  2¼ yd. of ¼" pale pink silk double-faced satin ribbon

4 pearl pink ⁵⁄₁₆" half-ball buttons

Helen Gibb's pink Vintage Brooch with Buds ribbonwork kit

5" of ¾" pink pleated trim (optional, for use with ribbonwork kit)

Other supplies and tools:
  2½ yd. of 20" white or ivory fusible knit interfacing

  54" x 44" piece of silk or cotton batting

  Iron and ironing board

  Sewing machine with basic machine embroidery ability plus basic accessories

Basic sewing supplies

Fabric scissors

Sewing threads: neutral and ivory

Machine embroidery threads: blush, medium and bright pink, light yellow

Water-soluble fabric marker

Loop turner tool

8½" x 11" sheets of all purpose paper for machine quilting/embroidery

Wildly Charming patterns: A, B, C, D, E, F, G, H, I, J, K

Finished size: Petite

Construction notes: The main elements of the quilt are worked in a four-step process. First, the fabrics are readied to be quilted. Second, the individual pieces are quilted. Third, the patterns are used to cut the quilted pieces. Fourth, the pieces are sewn together. Before cutting out the quilt pieces, read Prep the Pieces for Quilting.

CUT AND PREP THE PIECES FOR QUILTING

Cut the Pieces to be quilted ½" larger all around the pattern, unless otherwise indicated. Begin by pinning pattern pieces to the fabric. Then, add the ½" quilting allowance specified, using a water soluble fabric marker, drawing directly on the fabric. Cut out pieces of interfacing large enough to be applied to the fabric wrong side. Cut pieces of batting a bit larger than fabric pieces. Once the pieces are quilted, the actual pattern size is drawn onto the quilted piece, which is then stay stitched before being cut out. Use the Cutting Guide above when determining quantity of pieces to be cut.

Transfer all construction markings carefully to cut pieces.

CUTTING GUIDE

Asterisk (°) indicates pieces are interfaced.

Fabric	Pattern	Description	Quantity
Light pink dupioni	Bodice center front A	°Quilted with metallic overlay	Cut 1 on fold
	Skirt center front C	°Quilted	Cut 2 (l & r)
	Bodice side back G	°Quilted with metallic overlay	Cut 2 (l & r)
	Skirt center back H	°Quilted	Cut 2 (l & r)
	Bodice center back/ facing L		Cut 2

Fabric	Pattern	Description	Quantity
Blush dupioni	Skirt middle front D	°Quilted	Cut 2 (l & r)
	Skirt lower front F	°Quilted	Cut 1 on fold
	Skirt middle back I	°Quilted	Cut 2 (l & r)
Light Salmon shantung	Bodice side front B	°Quilted	Cut 2 (l & r)
	Skirt side front E	°Quilted	Cut 2 (l & r)
	Skirt side back J	°Quilted	Cut 2 (l & r)
Blush metallic crinkle	Bodice center front A overlay	7½" x 15"	Cut 1
	Bodice side back G overlay	6½" x 10½"	Cut 2
	Lower edge binding	1¾" x 30"	Cut 1
Off-white organza	Skirt lower front pleated overlay K	Not quilted	Cut 1 on fold
	Sash	4" x 35"	Cut 1
	Shoulder straps	2⅛" x 42"	Cut 1
Cream with black dot	Bodice center front A	For lining	Cut 1 on fold
	Bodice side front B	For lining	Cut 2 (l & r)
	Skirt center front C	For lining	Cut 2 (l & r)

Fabric	Pattern	Description	Quantity
	Skirt middle front D	For lining	Cut 2 (l & r)
	Skirt side front E	For lining	Cut 2 (l & r)
	Skirt lower front F	For lining	Cut 1 on fold
	Bodice side back G	For lining	Cut 2 (l & r)
	Skirt center back H	For lining	Cut 2 (l & r)
	Skirt middle back I	For lining	Cut 2 (l & r)
	Skirt side back J	For lining	Cut 2 (l & r)
	Binding strip	Cut size is 1½" x 25", on straight of grain, for lower edge of K	Cut 1
Cream with black dot	Piping strip	Cut size is 1½" x 30", on straight of grain, for empire waist	Cut 1
	¾"-wide bias strips	Bodice front bows (spaghetti) 14" long	Cut 2
		Front Knots (spaghetti) 14" long	Cut 1
		Bodice back loops (spaghetti) 20" long	Cut 1
		Skirt back loops (spaghetti) 8" long	Cut 1

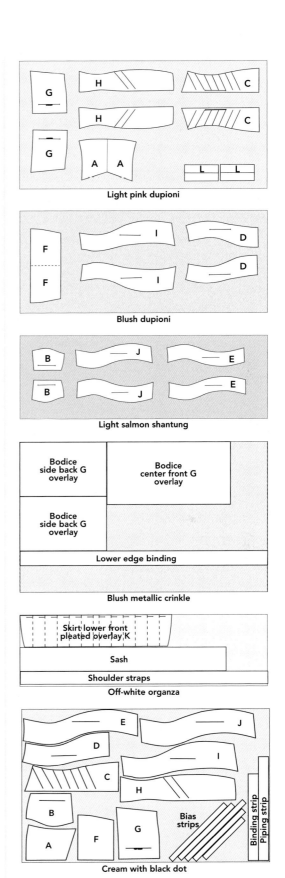

Cutting diagrams.

LIGHT PINK SILK

1 Using the water soluble fabric marker directly on the fabric, add ½" around pattern A bodice center front. Add ½" around two of the pattern C skirt center fronts (one left and one right facing), except along the center front edge. Add ½" around two of the pattern G bodice side backs (one left and one right facing). Add ½" around two of the pattern H skirt center backs (one left and one right facing), except along the center back edge. Cut out each piece, either on the drawn line or pattern line, as indicated in these directions. Cut two of the pattern L bodice center back facings on pattern lines. Cut and fuse interfacing to backsides of all pieces. Cut pieces of batting a bit larger than fabric for pieces A, C, G and H. Pin batting pieces to interface-side of fabric pieces.

BLUSH SILK

2 Using the water soluble fabric marker directly on the fabric, add a ½" around two of pattern D skirt middle fronts (one left and one right facing). Add a ½" around one pattern F skirt lower front (place piece on fabric fold). Add a ½" around two of pattern I skirt middle backs (one left and one right facing). Cut out each piece on the drawn lines. Cut and fuse interfacing to backsides of all pieces. Cut pieces of batting a bit larger than fabric for pieces D, F and I. Pin batting pieces to interface-side of fabric pieces.

LIGHT SALMON SILK

3 Using the water soluble fabric marker directly on the fabric, add a ½" around two of pattern B bodice side fronts (one left and one right facing). Add a ½" all around two of pattern E skirt side fronts (one left and one right facing). Add a ½" all around two of pattern J skirt side backs (one left and one right facing). Cut out each piece on the drawn lines. Cut and fuse interfacing to backsides of all pieces. Cut pieces of batting a bit larger than fabric for pieces B, E and J. Pin batting pieces to interfaced side of fabric pieces.

CUT THE OTHER FABRICS

4 Cut the blush metallic crinkle pieces as indicated in the cutting guide and cutting diagram.

5 Cut the off-white organza pieces as indicated in the cutting guide and cutting diagram.

6 Cut the cream with black dot pieces as indicated in the cutting guide and cutting diagram.

QUILT THE GARMENT PIECES

Seam allowance is ⅜" throughout unless otherwise noted.

7 Sew skirt center front C together, right sides facing, along center front edges. Sew skirt center back H together, right sides facing, beginning at dot along center back and sewing to hemline. Press seam allowances open.

8 Machine quilt on diagonal stitch lines indicated on the patterns, using a decorative embroidery stitch. Use blush machine embroidery thread for the task. You will need to place all-purpose paper on the batting sides before quilting with embroidery stitches. I used a single rosebud design that had an overall stitch length of 1" per repeat. I set the repeat at 4x and embroidery-quilted from the outer edge to the center for each row of stitching, then filled in along the center by embroidering down the center seam line as well, ending stitches at bottom row of embroidery for the front and at hem line for the back. You may wish to use a simple straight stitch for this task. Test stitches on scrap of fabric. Tear away paper once embroidery-quilting is complete.

9 Trace actual pattern C onto embroidered skirt center fronts and pattern K onto embroidered skirt center backs, allowing for the fact that the seam has already been sewn along centers. Machine sew a scant ⅛" inward from traced lines, then cut out on traced lines.

10 Machine-quilt pattern D skirt middle fronts and pattern I skirt middle backs with a rose and leaf pattern accomplished with the free-motion quilting technique. Use medium pink machine embroidery thread on the top and bright pink machine embroidery thread in the bobbin. Place all-purpose paper on the batting side of each piece before quilting with embroidery stitches. Tear away paper once embroidery-quilting is complete.

11 Machine-quilt pattern F skirt lower front in the same manner as step 10.

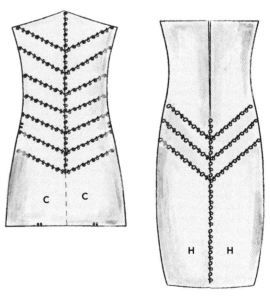

Quilt with machine embroidery stitch on the diagonal stitch lines shown on patterns C and H, beginning each row at the outer edge and working toward the center.

Construction notes: The sewing machine I used has a stitch regulator for free-motion quilting or embroidery, which allows me to use either a straight stitch or a zigzag stitch. I used the zigzag stitch option to create the free-motion embroidery design, with a stitch width of 1.9 and stitch depth of .04. If your machine does not have the zigzag stitch option, use the straight stitch to machine quilt the rose and leaf pattern with the free-motion technique. Test your movements and thread on scrap fabric to get a feel for the free-motion design.

Rose and leaf free-motion machine quilting/ embroidery pattern.

12 Trace actual pattern D onto embroidered skirt middle fronts and pattern I onto embroidered skirt middle backs. Trace pattern F skirt lower front, onto embroidered skirt lower front, flipping pattern at center in order to trace it's full-size. Machine sew a scant ⅛" inward from traced lines, then cut out on traced lines.

13 Machine-quilt pattern E skirt side fronts and pattern J skirt side backs with a melting chocolate swirling pattern accomplished with the free-motion quilting technique, using the light yellow machine embroidery thread. Paper backing is not needed for steps 13 or 14.

14 Machine-quilt pattern B bodice side fronts in the same manner as step 13.

15 Trace actual pattern E onto embroidered skirt side fronts, pattern J onto embroidered skirt side backs and pattern B onto bodice side fronts. Machine sew a scant ⅛" inward from traced lines, then cut out on traced lines.

SEW THE BODICE

Construction notes: All seam allowances are pressed open once a seam has been sewn.

16 Divide the blush metallic crinkle overlay piece for the bodice center front A into thirds horizontally, which can be accomplished by folding the piece of fabric. Sew double rows of machine gather stitches on each fold and along top and bottom edges. Pull threads to shirr metallic crinkle overlay piece.

Sew gather stitches horizontally on the blush metallic crinkle overlay piece.

17 Layer batting with Light Pink bodice center front A piece. Place shirred piece over light pink/batting bodice center front A. Adjust gathers evenly. Sew overlay to silk and batting with straight stitches along the middle horizontal rows. Remove gather stitches.

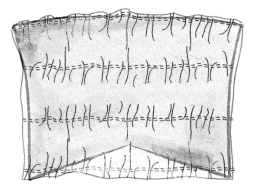

Sew shirred overlay along middle horizontal rows to silk/batting bodice center front.

18 Trace actual pattern A onto overlaid bodice center front, flipping pattern at center in order to trace its full size. Machine sew a scant ⅛" inward from traced lines, then cut out on traced lines.

19 Repeat steps 16 through 18 with bodice side back G silk, batting and metallic crinkle overlay pieces.

20 Fold one 14" length of ¾"-wide spaghetti in half, matching long edges. Sew down middle of strip. Insert loop turner tool into folded side of strip. Latch hook onto outer edge of fold at top of strip and pull on the tool so that the strip slips through folded side, turning strip right-side out, forming skinny spaghetti. Be gentle! Repeat for second 14" spaghetti strip. Repeat for all remaining spaghetti strips.

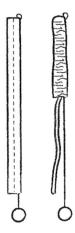

Sew spaghetti strip down the middle. Turn right-side out, using loop turner tool.

21 Tie a very small bow in the center of each 14" piece of spaghetti. Hand sew knot of bow to bodice center front along shirred rows, then extend spaghetti to side edges. Baste stitch in place.

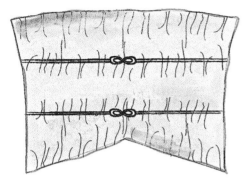

Sew bow knots to center front and extend spaghetti ends to side edges.

22 Cut ten 2" lengths from the 20" piece of spaghetti. Pin pieces in a U shape to the loop edges of the bodice side backs where indicated on pattern. Baste stitch loops in place.

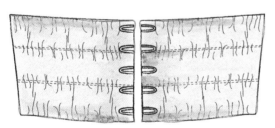

Baste stitch spaghetti loops to edges of bodice side back indicated on pattern.

23 Sew bodice center front to bodice side fronts, right sides facing, matching marks. Sew bodice side backs to front along side seams. Press seam allowances open.

24 Sew one long edge of bodice center back/facings L to loop edge of bodice side backs, right sides facing. Press seam allowance toward facing.

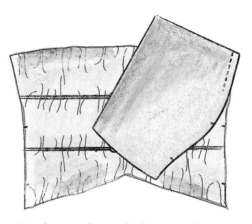

Matching marks, sew bodice center front to bodice side fronts.

MAKE THE ORGANZA FRONT KICK PLEAT

25 Press the 25" binding strip in half, matching long edges. Sew raw edges of strip to binding edge of skirt lower front pleated overlay K piece, using a scant ¼" seam allowance. Sew again ⅛" to the right of first row of stitching. Trim away excess past second row of stitching. Press binding downward, then wrap around to opposite side. Sew folded edge in place by machine or hand, enclosing the seam allowance.

26 To pleat overlay, fold and crisply press organza on dashed lines, then fold pressed edge to meet solid line, folding in the direction of the arrows, as indicated on the pattern. Press. Work one pleat at a time. Baste stitch pleats in place along upper edge.

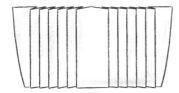

Fold and press crisp pleats on the organza, folding the pleats in the direction of the arrows shown on the pattern.

27 Pin and baste stitch pleated organza overlay to Skirt Lower Front F along upper edge.

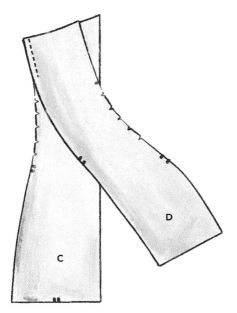

Sew curved edges together, clipping inward curves and matching marks. Stretch or ease pieces together when sewing.

SEW THE SKIRT

Construction notes: When sewing skirt pieces together, carefully clip all inward curves up to but not through seam line. Pin pieces together at matching marks and stretch or ease curved edges to fit, as needed.

28 Sew skirt center front C to skirt middle front D along side edges, right sides facing, matching marks. Press seam allowances open.

Sew skirt lower front F with kick pleat overlay to bottom edges of center/middle fronts, right sides facing, matching centers. Sew skirt side fronts E to outer edges of skirt middle fronts, right sides facing, matching marks. At the hem edge, leave the organza kick pleat free from the seam line for a space of about 1". It will be hand sewn in place a bit later. Press seam allowances open.

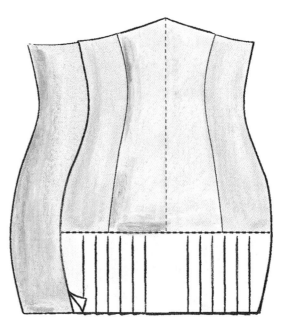

Fold the kick pleat away from seam line, about 1" from bottom of seam, not sewing that portion of organza into the seam line.

29 Sew skirt center back H to skirt middle backs I along side edges, right sides facing, matching marks. Press seam allowances open. Sew skirt side backs J to outer edge of skirt middle backs, right sides facing, matching marks. Press seam allowances open.

30 Sew skirt side backs to side fronts, right sides facing, matching marks. Press seam allowances open.

MAKE AND SEW SASH TO SKIRT

31 Sew a very narrow hem along one long edge of the organza sash strip. Press. Fold in half, matching short ends, to find center. Hand gather sash at fold so that the gathered center measures 1¼" wide including upper edge seam allowance. Secure gathers. Pin and baste stitch remaining long edge of sash to upper edge of skirt, placing wrong side of sash against right side of skirt. At center back, gather sash ends where it aligns with center back seam line, gathering sash down to 1⅝" with seam allowance. Baste stitch gathered edge in place at center back seam line.

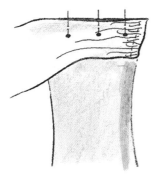

Gather sash at center back seam line so sash measures 1⅝" wide when gathered.

SEW PIPING TO SKIRT

32 Press 30" piping strip in half, matching long edges. Baste stitch raw edges of piping to upper edge of skirt, right sides facing, placing stitches 1/16" inward from the ⅜" seam allowance.

33 Cut four 2" lengths from the 8" piece of spaghetti. Pin pieces in a U shape to the left edge of the skirt center back where indicated on pattern. Baste stitch loops in place.

SEW THE LINING

34 Sew lining together in the same manner as for the outer pieces. Sew bodice together. Sew skirt together. Do not sew skirt to bodice at this time. Press all seam allowances open after completing each individual seam.

MAKE THE STRAPS

35 Working with the 2⅛"-wide organza shoulder strap piece, press one long edge over ⅝". Press the other long edge over ¼". Fold and press the ¼" edge over so it overlaps the ⅝" edge about ¼".

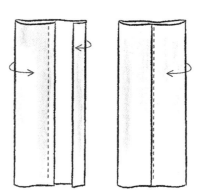

Press organza strip over ⅝" on one edge and ¼" on the other, then press the ¼" edge so it overlaps the ⅝" edge about ¼".

36 Machine gather-stitch down center of strip. Pull on thread so strip gathers very slightly. Machine sew ¼"-wide satin ribbon down center of slightly gathered organza strip using a utilitarian stitch in a small size. I used a stitch intended for gathering elastic, which looks very pretty. Cut two 12½" lengths for straps. Set straps aside for now.

SEW THE LINING TO GARMENT

37 Pin and sew skirt lining to skirt along one center back edge, right sides facing, matching sew-to marks along center back. Break stitching at dot. Reposition skirt and skirt lining in order to sew the other center back edge to dot. Clip fabrics to dot. Edge press. Turn right side out. Press and top stitch center back. Pin upper edge of skirt lining to upper edge of skirt, wrong sides facing.

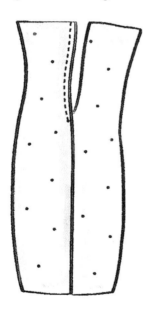

Sew skirt lining to skirt at center back, sewing to dot.

38 Sew lower edge of bodice to upper edge of lined skirt, right sides facing, matching center fronts and side seams. At back, skirt is sewn to bodice center back/facing dot only. Press seam allowance toward bodice.

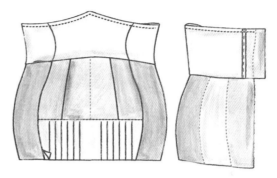

Sew bodice to skirt, matching center front and side seams. At back, sew skirt to facing dot.

39 Working from right side, fold piping upward onto bodice. Hand sew folded edge of piping onto lower edge of bodice.

40 Pin one end of each strap to upper edge of bodice center front/bodice side front seam line. Pin opposite ends to upper edge of bodice back where indicated on pattern. Baste stitch.

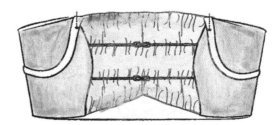

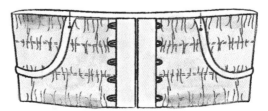

Pin straps to upper edge of bodice front and back.

41 Sew bodice lining to bodice, right sides facing, along top edge, sewing up to facing. Press seam allowance toward lining. Edge stitch seam allowance to lining. Fold lining down along seam line to inside and press.

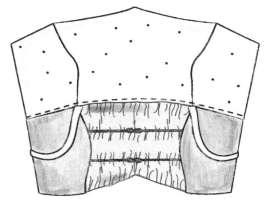

Edge stitch seam allowance to lining at seam line.

42 Smooth out bodice lining so lower edge aligns with bodice/skirt seam line. Turn lining raw edge under and pin over seam line, enclosing it. Hand sew lining in place.

43 Fold center back facing on fold line, right sides facing. Sew the top edge. Trim bulk from corner and turn facing right side out. Fold side and lower edges under, enclosing raw edges along bodice back and bodice/skirt seam line. Hand sew in place.

Fold facing back, right sides together. Sew the top edge.

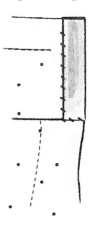

Fold facing to inside so that facing seam lines can be enclosed.

BIND THE BOTTOM EDGE

44 Pin together hem edges of skirt and skirt lining. Fold metallic crinkle strip in half, matching long edges. Sew raw edges to bottom edge of skirt/lining, making certain to not catch the organza kick pleat in the seam line when sewing. Sew again ⅛" to the right of first row of stitching. Trim away excess. Tightly wrap binding to inside. Pin and hand sew in place. Fold under and hand sew the "free" edges of organza kick pleat to side front seam line.

MAKE THE RIBBONWORK PIN AND OTHER FINISHING TOUCHES

45 Make the ribbonwork pin, following directions in Helen Gibb's pin kit. I substituted a bit of delicate, pleated pink trim for one of the steps, as I wanted a very minimal amount of green to be showing on the garment. Pin to upper right corner of organza kick pleat through all garment front layers.

46 Sew the pearl pink buttons to center back right side.

47 Thread remaining silk satin ribbon through bodice back loops, beginning at lower edge facing loops. Tie ribbon into a soft bow at upper edge and knot ribbon ends. Working with the remaining spaghetti, cut (5) 2½" lengths. Tie small knots centered on each length, then trim both ends at a slant, about ⅝" from knot. Sew knots to center front, beginning just below gathered edge of sash and spacing the knots about 1½" apart. Ta Da!

Almost Famous

AS OUR KIDS HAVE GOTTEN OLDER, living in places of their own, we have continued to receive some of their mail. What to do with it all without adding to our own clutter, that's the question. We decided upon a small organizer. The one we have is too small, really. I'd love to use this three-pouch organizer to resolve cluttering issues.

MATERIALS

Silk fabrics:
  One 7½" x 10½" piece silk dupioni or shantung for each of the following shades: Light brown, spice, pumpkin, tangerine, heliotrope and pansy

  18" x 10" piece of silk gold metallic crinkle

  ¾ yd. 44"-wide lavender blush silk dupioni

Embellishments:
  4 yd. purple 7mm silk ribbon

  1½ yd. of Gold 7mm silk ribbon

  1½ yd. of light gold 4mm silk ribbon

  1 yd. bright heliotrope 1½"-wide ribbon

1 yd. of gold and rust variegated 1½" ribbon

About 12 large, amber or amethyst beads in assorted sizes and shapes

About 16 round or faceted round 4mm amber or amethyst beads

About 100 size 11 assorted gold, amethyst or amber seed beads

Other supplies and tools:
  2 yd. of 20"-wide white or ivory fusible knit interfacing

  9½" x 24" piece of fleece or needle punch batting

  Iron and ironing board

  Sewing machine with basic accessories

Basic sewing supplies

Self-healing cutting mat

Rotary cutter

Grid lined ruler

Size 20 chenille needle

Size 3 embroidery needle

Beading or milliner's needle

Fabric scissors

Sewing threads: taupy brown

Wildly Charming patterns: A, B, C, D, E, F, G

Three images of vintage ladies, printed on cotton, each about 3" x 2¼" (optional)

Finished size: 9½" wide x 26" long

CUTTING GUIDE

Fabric	Pattern	Description	Quantity	Fabric	Pattern	Description	Quantity
Interfacing:	#1–6 fabrics	Cut size is 7½" x 10½"	6 pieces	Heliotrope dupioni	Flap C	Pieced	Cut 1
	Flap top strip B	See pattern	Cut 2 from right side, 1 from reverse	Pansy dupioni	Flap C (reverse)	Pieced	Cut 2
	Pouch side pleat D	Pieced	6 pieces	Gold metallic crinkle	Flap top strip B	Pieced	Cut 1 from right side, 2 from reverse
	Pouch lining E	Pieced	3 pieces		Ruffle strip	Cut size is 3" x 18"	Cut 1
	Flap lining F	See pattern	Cut 2 from right side, 1 from reverse		Rod Pocket strip	Cut size is 3" x 18"	Cut 1
	Pouch back	Pieced	3 pieces	Lavender Blush dupioni	Backing	Cut size is 11½" x 24"	Cut 1
Fusible fleece:	Backing	Cut size is 9½" x 24"	1 piece		Pouch side pleat D	Pieced	Cut 6
Silks:					Pouch lining E	Cut size is 7" x 11½"	Cut 3
Light Brown shantung	Pouch stripe A	Pieced	Cut 4		Flap lining F	See pattern	Cut 2 from right side, 1 from reverse
Spice dupioni	Pouch stripe A	Pieced	Cut 4		Pouch back G	Cut size is 8⁵⁄₁₆" x 9½"	Cut 3
Pumpkin dupioni	Pouch stripe A	Pieced	Cut 4				
Tangerine dupioni	Pouch stripe A	Pieced	Cut 3				

CUT FABRICS

1 Apply interfacing to wrong sides of light brown shantung and spice, pumpkin, tangerine, heliotrope and pansy dupioni.

2 Cut 4 each of Pouch Stripe A from light brown shantung, spice and pumpkin dupioni, as shown in the diagram below.

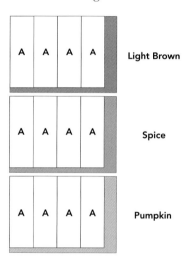

Cutting diagram for light brown shantung and spice and pumpkin dupioni.

3 Cut 3 of Pouch Stripe A from tangerine dupioni.

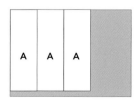

Cutting diagram for tangerine dupioni.

4 Cut 1 of Flap piece C, right side up, from heliotrope dupioni.

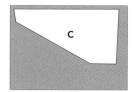

Cutting diagram for heliotrope dupioni.

5 Cut 2 of Flap piece C, reverse side up, from Pansy dupioni

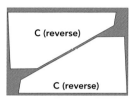

Cutting diagram for Pansy dupioni.

6 Cut 1 of Flap Top strip B, right side up and 2 of B, reverse side up, from gold metallic crinkle. Cut one 3" x 18" ruffle and one 3" x 18" rod pocket strip. Fuse interfacing to wrong sides of B's.

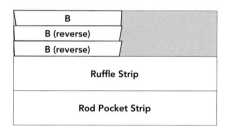

Cutting diagram for gold metallic crinkle.

7 From the lavender blush dupioni, cut one backing piece 11½" x 24", six Pouch side pleat D pieces, three Pouch lining E pieces, two Flap lining F pieces from right side and one reverse. Cut three Pouch back G pieces. Fuse interfacing to wrong sides of all pieces, except backing.

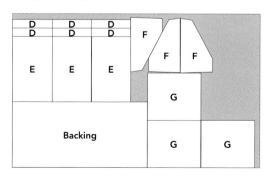

Cutting diagram for lavender blush dupioni.

PIECE THE POUCHES

All seam allowances are ¼" unless otherwise noted.

8 For upper pouch, sew five A's together, right sides facing, in this order: light brown, spice, pumpkin, tangerine, pumpkin. Sew a Pouch side pleat D to left and right edges of sewn-together A's. Press seam allowances open.

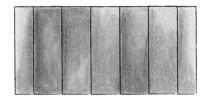

Sew light brown, spice, pumpkin, tangerine and pumpkin A pieces together for upper pouch. Sew a D piece to side edges.

9 For middle pouch, sew A's together as above in this order: spice, light brown, pumpkin, tangerine, light brown. Sew Pouch side pleat D to left and right edges, as above. Press seam allowances open.

10 For lower pouch, sew A's together in this order: spice, tangerine, light brown, pumpkin, spice. Sew Pouch side pleat D to left and right edges, as above. Press seam allowances open.

11 For each pouch, sew the 7mm purple silk ribbon over four A seam lines, using a narrow serpentine stitch.

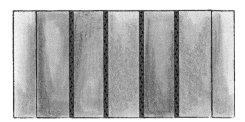

Use a narrow serpentine stitch to sew 7mm silk ribbon over four pouch seam lines.

MAKE THE FLAPS

12 For the upper and lower flaps, sew the reverse-cut flap top strips B to reverse-cut flap pieces C (pansy), right sides facing, matching marks. For the middle flap, sew right side-cut flap top strip B to right side-cut flap piece C (heliotrope), right sides facing, matching marks. Press seam allowances open.

Sew the reverse-side cuts of B and C together for upper and lower flaps. Sew right-side cuts of B and C together for middle flap.

13 If you have chosen three vintage images for the flaps, cut them out with an arch shape. It's okay if the sizes of the three images vary. Position images on flaps and machine sew in place along outer edge of image.

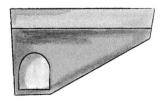

Machine sew arch-shaped images to flaps.

14 For folded ribbon triangles, cut eight 4" lengths from 1½" bright heliotrope ribbon. Cut seven pieces 4" wide from 1½" gold and rust variegated ribbon. If ribbon is wired, remove from selvages. Fold ribbon lengths diagonally as shown in diagrams. Press folds, but test iron temperature on scrap of ribbon first.

Fold one ribbon end diagonally forward. Fold opposite end diagonally forward, forming ribbon triangles. Press folds. Side showing is right side of triangle.

15 Pin triangles to lower edge of flaps, right side up, alternating ribbon shades. Use three bright-heliotrope and two gold and rust variegated for the upper and lower flaps. Use two bright heliotrope and three gold and rust for the middle flap. Pin triangles so that selvage edge of ribbon on underside will be caught in with the ¼" seam allowance when flap lining is sewn to flap in step 16.

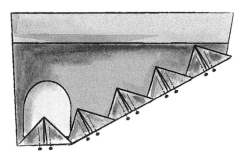

Alternating shades, pin folded ribbon triangles to lower edge of flaps.

16 Sew flap lining to flap, right sides facing, along sides and lower edge. Clip bulk from corners. Edge-press seam allowance open. Turn right-side out. Push out corners. At this point, the ribbon triangles will extend outward from the lower edge. The tips will be sewn up onto flap a bit later.

EMBELLISH THE FLAPS

17 Now is the time to embellish flaps. Pin 7mm purple silk ribbon to left or right edge of vintage image, then drape ribbon in a meandering fashion. Hand tack ribbon here and there along meandering edges.

18 Embroider around the ribbon with 7mm gold silk ribbon, using the Loop Petal stitch and 4mm light-gold silk ribbon, using the ribbon stitch. For the embroidery, there is no set design, so embroider in a random fashion.

RIBBON EMBROIDERY BASICS

NEEDLES

A chenille needle has a large eye and sharp point. It is used for embroidering with wider ribbon, such as the 7mm.

Standard embroidery needles, sizes 1 – 5, are used for embroidering with narrow ribbon, such as the 4mm. A size 1 needle has quite a thick shaft. Needle thickness decrease as needle number size increases (size 1 – larger than size 5). Generally, I use a size 3 embroidery needle for ribbon.

THREAD RIBBON ON NEEDLE

Cut ribbon end at a slant. Thread end through eye, then sew needle tip through ribbon about ¼" inward from end. Pull long ribbon end until short end "locks" onto needle at eye.

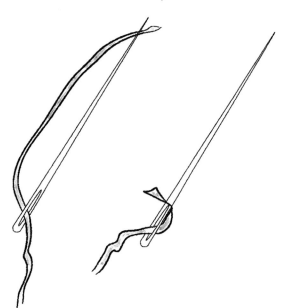

Lock short end of ribbon onto needle.

MAKE A SOFT KNOT

At long end, fold ribbon over on itself for a space of about ⅛". Sew needle through doubled ribbon fold and pull needle through. Slide "knot" down length of ribbon gently to end.

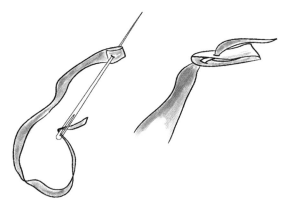

Make a soft knot at long ribbon end.

RIBBON STITCH

Bring ribbon to surface. Smooth under ribbon with needle at entry point to broaden ribbon. Extend ribbon on surface, allowing a bit of slack so ribbon is not flat against surface. Sew needle into ribbon at desired length of stitch (usually ¼" to ½") and pull ribbon through gently until tip of stitch makes a soft, little point.

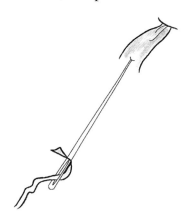

Ribbon stitch.

LOOP PETAL STITCH

Bring ribbon to surface, smooth underneath ribbon with needle at entry point. Extend ribbon on surface, then fold it back on itself for a length of about ¼". Sew back into ribbon loop and fabric just before original entry point. Stop sewing when tip of stitch forms a soft point.

Loop Petal Stitch.

19 Sew assorted seed beads to embroidery and meandering ribbon. Hand sew tips of ribbon triangles up onto flap fronts.

SEW FLAPS TO POUCHES

20 Place upper and lower pouches with corresponding flap. Place middle pouch with remaining flap.

21 Pin upper edge of flap to upper edge of pouch, having wrong side of flap against right side of pouch and centering flap .

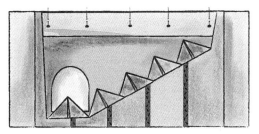

Pin wrong side of flap to right side of pouch centered along upper edges.

22 Pin and sew pouch lining E to layered flap and pouch, right sides together, along upper edge. Press seam allowance toward pouch. Fold lining to pouch backside, press. Edge-stitch pouch and lining, keeping flap free from stitching. After doing this, the flap will fold downward nicely. Pin pouch and lining layers together along raw edges. Repeat for each pouch, flap, and pouch lining.

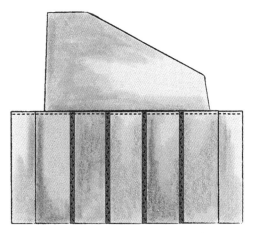

Edge stitch upper edge of pouch and lining.

SEW POUCHES TOGETHER

23 Place one pouch back on work surface, right side up, with 9½" edges at top and bottom. Align side edges of upper pouch with side edges of pouch back while matching up the bottom edges of each piece. Pouch bottom edge is wider than pouch back at this point. Sew side edges together.

24 Make a ½" deep pleat with the pouch side pleat section and pin pleat at bottom edges.

After sewing pouch side edges to pouch back, pin ½" deep pleats at sides along bottom edge.

25 Working with the second pouch back piece, pin lower edge to bottom edges of upper pouch/pouch back, right sides facing. Sew across bottom edge, then flip pouch back downward, forming the pouch back for the middle section. Sew middle pouch in place as in steps 23 and 24. Sew the lower pouch in the same manner.

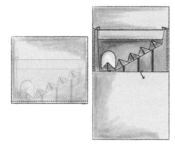

Sew second pouch back to bottom edges of first section.

BACK AND BIND THE QUILT

26 Place backing on your work surface, right side up. Place fleece or batting centered onto backing. Place pouch strip centered onto fleece. Machine sew pouch strip to fleece/backing along pouch back seam lines, using a straight or decorative stitch. Wrap side edge of backing over onto side edges of pouch strip. Turn backing raw edges under so that folded edge aligns with side edges of pouch strip. Machine sew binding in place.

MAKE THE BOTTOM RUFFLE

27 Working with the gold metallic crinkle ruffle strip, sew a narrow hem along the two short ends, then sew a narrow hem along one long edge. Press. Sew 2 rows of gathering stitches along the remaining long edge. Pull thread to gather strip. Pin gathered edge to bottom edge of pouch Strip. Sew in place.

28 Fold bottom edge of backing under and then over onto bottom edge of pouch strip. Sew in place, enclosing pouch and Ruffle raw edges. Press Ruffle downwards.

Sew ruffle to bottom edge of pouch strip.

MAKE THE ROD POCKET

29 Working with the Gold metallic crinkle Rod Pocket strip, sew a narrow hem along the 2 short ends. Press under one long edge and sew two rows of gathering stitches close to folded edge. Sew 2 rows of gathering stitches along remaining long edges on seam line.

30 Pull thread to gather side of strip with seam allowance. Pin and sew to upper edge of top pouch back piece through all layers. Sew again ⅛" to the right of first row of stitching. Trim away excess fabric from top. Overcast seam allowance.

31 Pull threads to gather folded edge of strip. Wrap strip around to backside. Pin and hand sew gathered edge to upper seam line, enclosing seam allowance. Leave sides open, as strip is now a rod pocket.

FINISH WITH BEAD DANGLES

32 Using the assorted sizes and shapes of the large beads, the 4mm round or faceted beads and the seed beads, sew two bead dangles of various length to shorter edge of each flap. Along bottom edge of pouch strip, tack right side of ruffle up onto side binding edge.

Spread Your Wings

BUTTERFLIES INSPIRE US. They are fascinating, helping us imagine angel wings. A butterfly reminds me of the myriad of times I've been allowed a second chance. I hope these ethereal, butterfly-shaped pillows have done the beautiful butterfly justice.

MATERIALS

Side-facing Butterfly Pillow

Silk fabrics:
  6" strip of 44" dove silk dupioni

  7" x 22" piece of dusk silk dupioni

  6" x 22" piece of willow silk dupioni

  7½" x 10½" piece of celery silk dupioni

  8" x 11½" piece of lavender blush silk dupioni

Embellishments:
  2½ yd. of 2½"-wide lavender and green variegated bias cut silk ribbon

  Aqua embroidery floss

  2 yd. narrow light-olive satin cording

Other supplies and tools:
  1 yd. 20"-wide lightweight knit fusible interfacing

  ⅓ yd. silk or cotton batting

  Size 5 embroidery needle

Open-winged Butterfly Pillow

Silk fabrics:
  ⅓ yd. 44" willow silk dupioni

  6" x 44" piece of lavender blush silk dupioni

  ½ yd. 42"–54" off-white silk organza

Embellishments:
  1¾ yd. 1½"-wide lavender and green variegated bias cut silk ribbon

  Clear iridescent and pewter-colored sequins

Other supplies and tools:
  1 yd. 20"-wide lightweight knit fusible interfacing

  10½" x 30" piece of silk or cotton batting

  Pinking shears

For both Butterfly Pillows

Embellishments:
  Packaged grouping of plum and blue assorted seed beads

1 pipe cleaner for each butterfly

Other supplies and tools:
  12 oz. of fiberfill for each butterfly

  Iron and ironing board

  Blank newsprint paper

  Sewing machine with basic machine embroidery ability plus basic accessories

  Basic sewing supplies

  Beading or milliner's needle

  Fabric scissors

  Sewing threads: neutral or matching

  Machine embroidery thread: Oyster white

  Instant set fabric dyes (optional)

  Patterns Spread Your Wings, side-facing butterfly: #1, 2, 3, 4, 5

  Patterns Spread Your Wings, open-winged butterfly: A, B, C, D

Finished sizes: Side-facing Butterfly 12" wide x 18" tall
Open-winged Butterfly 18" wide x 12" tall

Side-Facing Butterfly

CUTTING GUIDE

Asterisk (*) indicates piece is interfaced.

Fabric	Pattern	Description
Dove dupioni	#1	*Cut one left and one right facing
	For "rosebud" body	Tear a 6" x 22" strip
Dusk dupioni	#2	*Cut one left and one right facing
Willow dupioni	#3	*Cut one left and one right facing
Celery dupioni	#4	*Cut one left and one right facing
Lavender blush dupioni	#5	*Cut one left and one right facing

Open-Winged Butterfly

CUTTING GUIDE

Asterisk (*) indicates piece is interfaced.

Fabric	Pattern	Description
Lavender Blush dupioni	Upper wing A	*Cut one left and one right facing
	For "rosebud" body	Tear a 6" x 22" strip
Willow dupioni	Lower wing B	*Cut one left and one right facing
	Back C	*Cut one left and one right facing
Off-white organza	Wing petal D	Trace 42 (after embroidery)

CUT FABRICS – EITHER BUTTERFLY

Pattern notes: The paper patterns included in this book are sturdy enough to be used for pressing to create a finished edge for appliqué, in the same manner as would freezer paper patterns. With this in mind, the paper patterns serve two purposes: to use as a cutting pattern and to use as an edge for pressing. For both butterflies, dotted edges on patterns indicate those edges are to be prepared for appliqué. Edges without any markings indicate a ¼" underlap allowance. Edges with dashed lines indicate an outer edge with ⅜" seam allowance added. Cut out paper patterns very cleanly along dotted edges so that pattern can be adequately used for appliqué prep process.

For appliqué patterns, hand draw an additional ¼" appliqué allowance on fabric along appliqué edge. You will cut fabric on the hand drawn edges.

1 Cut fabrics for side-facing or open-winged butterflies, as described in the Cutting Guide. Cut required interfacing for those pieces indicated by an asterisk (*). Fuse interfacing to wrong sides of all necessary pieces.

Side-Facing Butterfly

Construction notes: Each pattern for the side-facing butterfly has 2 cut pieces, one that is left facing and one that is right facing. When preparing the pieces for appliqué, work the left facing piece and then reverse the process for the right facing piece.

PREPARE EDGES FOR APPLIQUE

2 Place #2 wing pattern, wrong side up, on Dusk wing fabric piece, interfaced side up. Using a steam iron, press outer raw edge of fabric up and over onto paper pattern along dotted edge indicated on pattern. Clip inward curves when pressing, being careful to not form points along edges when pressing. Use a bit of water spray if necessary to achieve a crisp edge. Remove paper pattern. Press fabric edges again from both the interfaced and right sides. This is the left facing, or front, #2 wing piece. Reverse and prepare the other #2, or back, wing piece for appliqué.

3 Repeat step 2 above for #3, #4 and #5 wing patterns.

4 Beginning with the front side, overlap #2 wing piece onto #1 wing piece along the underlap allowance. Pin and machine sew in place, using a narrow decorative stitch. Test stitch styles and size options on scrap fabric first. The serpentine stitch size I used had a width of 1.5 and a depth of 1.5, making the stitch small and unobtrusive, yet effective. Repeat for back side.

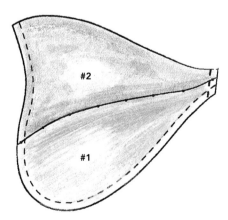

Machine appliqué #2 wing piece onto #1 wing piece for both the left and right, or front and back, facing sides.

5 Repeat step 4 with remaining wing pieces, for both the front and back sides, working the pieces in numerical order.

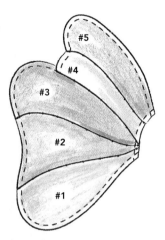

Machine appliqué the remaining wing pieces, working in numerical order.

6 Cut 2 pieces of batting ½" larger around than assembled wing size. Layer batting under wrong sides of front and back wings.

7 Using 2 different, large-sized decorative stitches, machine embroider wings, adding subtle texture. Press carefully. Trim excess batting.

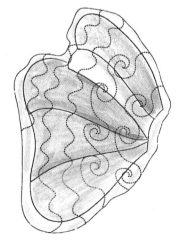

Machine embroider larger-sized decorative stitches on front and back wings.

DYEING OPTIONS

8 When I got to this point in the construction process, I thought I'd try experimenting with some instant set dyes formulated for silk or wool, both protein fabrics, to which I'd recently been introduced. Of course, dyeing is a whole world unto itself, so I'll touch marginally on the topic. Instant set dyes work with cold water and can be used very diluted or full strength and everything in-between. Mostly, I worked with the dyes quite diluted, applying them to the wings along seam lines and outer edges with a paint brush. I also dyed the rose-bud body fabric piece at the same time. My goal was to achieve subtle shading, which I did. The great thing about the instant set dyes is that the dyed fabric needs no rinsing. I was quite anxious to see the finished results, so I pressed the dyed wings and body fabric dry. If you are interested in achieving the same result, I suggest you look into purchasing some instant set dyes and giving them a try.

SEW FRONT AND BACK

9 Sew front and back wings together, right sides facing, using ⅜" seam allowance, leaving the inner or body edge not sewn. Trim seam allowance to ¼" and clip inward and outward curves and inner points. Edge press seam allowance open. Turn right side out.

10 Stuff butterfly with fiberfill through body edge. Turn body raw edges inward and whip stitch opening closed.

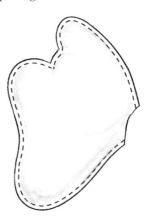

Sew front to back.

ADD SATIN CORD DETAILING

11 Swirl the satin cording into a spiral shape near the top outer edge of the front upper wing, meandering the cording around to the backside. Pin the cording in place here and there. Use two strands of the embroidery floss to couch-stitch cording in place. Meander the cording near the middle of the lower wing on the front side and couch-stitch in place.

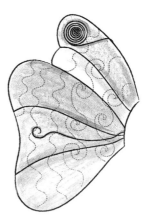

Meander the satin cording in spirals and couch stitch in place, using embroidery floss.

ADD RUCHED RIBBON

12 Cut the ½"-wide bias cut silk ribbon into three equal lengths. Fold one length in half, matching cut edges, but do not press. Sew one row of machine gathering stitches ¼" inward from raw edges through both layers. Pull thread to gather ribbon slightly.

Machine gather-stitch ¼" inward from raw edges.

13 Beginning at front "body" edge, pin gathered ribbon to appliqué seam line that is between #2 and #3 appliqué pieces, adjusting gathers and wrapping ribbon from the front, around to butterfly back. Hand sew ribbon in place while beading it along gathering stitch line. Use the milliner's or beading needle for the duo task.

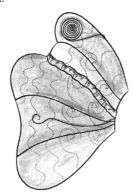

Hand sew while beading the gathered ribbon in place.

13 Repeat for the other two lengths of ribbon, placing one gathered length on the seam line that is between # 3 and #4 applique pieces and the other length on the seam line that is between #4 and #5 appliqué pieces.

MAKE ROSEBUD-SHAPED BODY

15 Cut pipe cleaner so it is 8" in length and bend a ½" loop at one end.

16 Working with the 22" x 6" piece of dove dupioni and following the diagram below, make the butterfly's "rosebud" body. The fabric edges are kept unfinished.

Fold right end diagonally forward. Sew pipe cleaner loop to fabric near fold (a). Fold fabric over (b).

Roll folded edge to just past end of second diagonal fold (c), forming a coiled center. Tack at bottom edge.

Fold fabric diagonally to the back and roll upper edge of coiled center onto diagonal fold (d). Tack at bottom edge.

Start wrapping remaining fabric around pipe cleaner (e). Tack the fabric invisibly in place every so often to keep fabric from unwrapping. At end, fold raw edges under and tack in place.

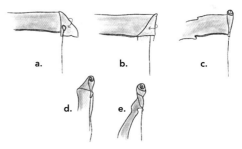

Making the butterfly's rosebud body.

17 Pin rosebud body to body edge of wings centered over the hand sewn seam. Invisibly tack body over seam. You will need to work the needle from front and back in a back and forth manner. Bend body slightly so that tip can be sewn to front of wings on the #1 applique piece.

FINISH THE ROSEBUD-SHAPED BODY

18 Make the body for the butterfly from the 22" x 6" piece of lavender blush dupioni, as was done in steps 14 and 15 for the Side-Facing Butterfly.

19 Pin body centered to butterfly front. Invisibly tack body over seam. Bend body so that tip can be sewn at a slight curve to butterfly back.

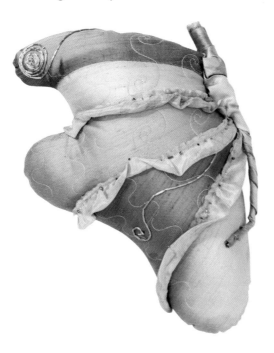

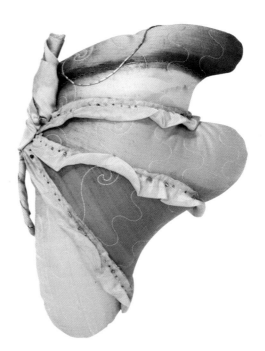

Open-Winged Butterfly

EMBROIDERING THE WING PETALS

1 Refer to Cutting Guide on page 108 and step 1 for the Side-Facing Butterfly pillow.

2 Press silk organza in half, matching selvage edges. Pin blank newsprint paper to underside of double-layered organza. Using decorative stitches, machine embroider the silk organza piece with oyster white embroidery thread, working from four to seven randomly curved rows on fabric with the stitches. If desired, different stitches can be used for each row. The embroidery creates a very subtle effect and not all wing petals will have bits of embroidery. Before embroidering, test desired stitches on scrap fabric.

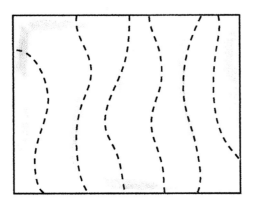

Machine embroider 4 to 7 randomly curved rows of decorative stitches on the double-layered piece of silk organza.

3 Tear away newsprint paper from embroidered organza. The porous nature of this paper makes the tear-away process easy. Use your fingernail or a straight pin to pick-out paper from some of the smaller embroidered areas. Press organza.

4 Trace 42 wing petal pattern D's onto right side of embroidered organza, leaving a ¼" space between each and using a pencil lightly for tracing. Machine sew around curved edges, but not straight edge, using the serpentine stitch with a depth of 1mm and width of 1mm. Cut wing petals out, using pinking shears, just to the outside of stitched lines and directly on straight lines. Press petals again.

EMBROIDER THE WINGS

5 Cut 2 pieces of batting ½" larger all around than upper wing A, lower wing B and back C. Layer batting under wrong sides of corresponding fabric pieces.

6 Using 2 different decorative stitches, similarly to step 7 for Side-Facing Butterfly, machine embroider wings, adding subtle texture. Press carefully. Trim excess batting.

PLACE ORGANZA PETALS ON LOWER WINGS

7 Working with lower wing B pieces, pin wing petals, right side up, onto right sides of lower wings, placing the wing petals in the numerical order shown in the diagram. Sew the wing petals in place along straight edges only. Petals along outer edges will extend off lower wing pieces.

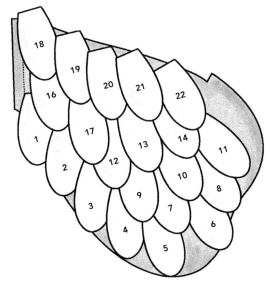

Pin and sew wing petals to lower wing pieces, placing them in the numerical order shown.

SEW UPPER WINGS TO LOWER WINGS

8 Prepare the upper wing A fabric pieces for appliqué along dotted edge indicated on pattern, with the same approach as in step 2 for Side-Facing Butterfly. Clip fabric to dot indicated on pattern when working the edge for appliqué.

9 Pin upper wings onto lower wings on the dashed overlap line indicated on pattern. Machine sew in place.

10 Sew left and right upper wings together, right sides facing, along center front. Press seam allowance open.

Dyeing Options: If desired, now is the time to dye the front and back wings. Read through step 8 above for Side-Facing Butterfly to help with your decision.

SEW FRONT TO BACK

11 Working with the back C pieces, press center back edges under ⅜". Pin front wings to back, right sides facing, aligning outer wing edges. Make certain to pin the wing petals up and away from the seam line before sewing, so they do not get caught up in the stitching. Sew front to back, using ⅜" seam allowance. Clip all curves and inward points. Edge press. Turn right side out. Stuff with fiberfill through center back opening. Hand sew opening closed.

EMBELLISH WITH RIBBON, SEQUINS AND BEADS

12 Hand sew sequins and beads to some wing petals. Sew small clusters of sequins and beads to upper wings near outer edges.

13 Cut the 1½"-wide bias cut silk ribbon into two equal lengths. Fold one length in half, matching cut edges, but do not press. Sew one row of machine gathering stitches ¼" inward from raw edges through both layers. Pull thread to gather ribbon slightly. Pin and hand sew ribbon to upper wings similarly as was done in step 12 for the Side-Facing Butterfly.

Natural Beauty

THIS LUSCIOUS LINGERIE BAG has been sized to rest comfortably among many bed pillows. Yet it is a piece that is both clever and useful as a hideaway. The Knotted Mum gracing the front is a favorite ribbonwork technique of mine.

MATERIALS

Silk fabrics:
  18" x 22" piece of plum/ teal variegated hand dyed silk velvet

  ½ yd. 44"-wide lavender blush silk dupioni

  1 yd. 44"-wide willow silk dupioni

Embellishments:
  ¾ yd. 2½"-wide periwinkle/ coral/light olive variegated bias cut silk ribbon

2 yd. each of ⁷⁄₁₆"-wide bias cut silk ribbon in the following shades (knotted mum): Lavender, periwinkle and medium-green variegated, Light-purple/ yellow variegated, Light-lime variegated, Olive variegated (ties, ribbon drape)

Beaded button or cluster for flower center

Other supplies and tools:
  26" x 18" piece of wool batting

Iron and ironing board

Sewing machine plus basic accessories

Basic sewing supplies

Hand sewing needle

Fabric scissors

Sewing threads: neutral or matching

Finished size: 16"-wide x 12" (folded in half)

CUTTING GUIDE

Fabric	Cut size	Description
Hand dyed velvet	8" x 17"	Lower Front, cut 1
	7" x 17"	Small Pocket, cut 2
Lavender Blush dupioni	27" x 18"	Upper Front/ Back cut 1
	8" x 17"	Small Pocket Lining, cut 2
Willow dupioni	13" x 17"	Lining, cut 2
	23" x 17"	Large Pocket, cut 2

MAKE THE LINING AND INNER POCKETS

All seam allowances are ½" unless otherwise noted.

1 Sew the two lining pieces together along one 17" edge, right sides facing, leaving a 10" opening in order to turn the lingerie bag right side out at a later step.

2 Press the two large pockets in half, wrong sides facing, matching the 17" edges. Sew one velvet small pocket to one dupioni small pocket lining along one 17" edge, right sides facing. Press seam allowance toward dupioni. Fold dupioni in order to align remaining 17" edges, wrong sides facing. The dupioni will create a band for the velvet pocket. Pin outer edges together.

3 Place lining on work surface, right side up. Place large pockets onto lining, matching outer edges. Place small pockets over large pockets, matching outer edges. Pin layers together. Mark center of pockets. Sew pockets to lining along center mark. Baste stitch outer edges of all layers together.

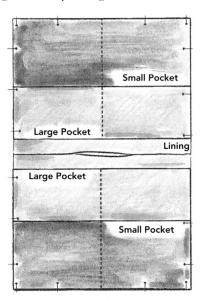

Small Pocket

Large Pocket

Lining

Large Pocket

Small Pocket

Pin large and small pockets to lining.
Sew middle of pockets to lining.

SHIRRING THE SILK

4 To mark lavender blush upper front/back piece for shirring, press piece in half, matching the 27" edges. Open-out fabric. From the center mark, press again at 2¾" intervals from both sides of center, being careful to not un-press center mark. The last intervals along side edges will measure 3½" wide.

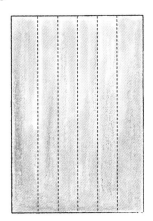

Press upper front/back at 2¾" intervals to mark piece for shirring.

5 Sew rows of gathering stitches along each pressed mark, sewing a double row of stitches and spacing stitches a scant ⅛" apart. Sew two rows of gathering stitches along the outer side edges too, placing first row at the ½" seam line and second row a scant ⅛" to the right of, or inward from, the first.

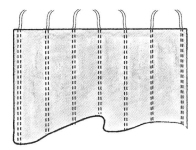

Sew double rows of gathering stitches along each pressed mark and at outer edges.

6 To ruche piece, gently pull threads from one side of the fabric, pulling the two threads simultaneously along one pressed mark at a time. When each row has been gathered down, the Upper Front/Back needs to measure 19" in ruched length. The 17" width will not change. Knot thread ends together at each mark on both the top and bottom edges, once ruched piece is 19" in length.

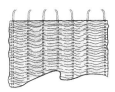

Pull gently on the gathering threads to ruche upper front/back piece.

SEW THE OUTER COVER

7 Place batting on your work surface. Pin ruched upper front/back to batting, aligning one 17" to batting and with the upper front/back piece centered along the batting sides. Sew the upper front/back to the batting along all inner ruched rows, using a narrow decorative stitch. I used one of my favorites, the serpentine stitch, with a width of 1.5 and a length of 1.5. Do not sew outer rows to batting at this time.

Construction notes: I did not need to remove the shirring stitches, as they did not interfere with the overall look. But, if desired, remove shirring stitches.

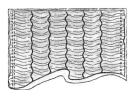

Sew ruched piece to batting along the inner shirred rows, using a decorative stitch.

8 Fold the 2½"-wide bias cut ribbon in half, matching long, raw edges and sew two rows of gathering stitches along edges. Pull thread to gather ribbon to a length of 17". Pin gathered edge of ribbon to one 17" edge of velvet, right sides facing.

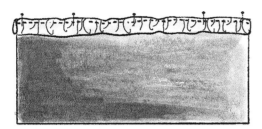

Pin gathered ribbon to one 17" velvet edge.

9 Pin and sew ribbon edge of velvet to quilted upper front and back along the edge with the large amount of excess batting. Hand-press velvet downward. Pin and baste all outer edges to batting, using a ⅜" seam allowance. Trim excess batting.

ASSEMBLE THE LINGERIE BAG

10 Pin lining to outer piece, right sides together. Sew along all edges. Trim bulk from corners. Edge press seam allowances open. Turn right-side out through lining opening. Lightly press from lining side. Hand sew lining opening closed.

MAKE THE KNOTTED MUM FLOWER

11 Set aside the olive variegated ribbon for now.

12 Knot a length of doubled thread. Working with the remaining ⁷⁄₁₆" bias cut ribbons, cut the entire length of each into 5" pieces. Tie a tight knot at exact center of each length (a). Fold a length in half, matching cut ends. Begin sewing gathering stitches about ¼" inward from cut ends (b). Don't knot thread. Fold second length in half and gather stitch across cut ends, chaining the second to the first. Continue to chain gather-stitch the folded lengths together, working with the different colors randomly (c). It's helpful to sit when doing this task and to use your legs as a work surface. You will be working with a lot of loops, so try to keep them all facing the same direction.

a.

b.

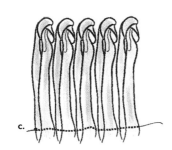

c.

Knotted Mum.

13 Join the last loop to the first and securely knot thread. Adjust loops. Sew a beaded button or cluster of beads or anything of your choice to flower center.

FINISHING TOUCHES

14 Cut two 24" lengths from the olive variegated ribbon. Hand sew the center of each length to the inside of the bag about 1" inward from upper and lower edges on pocket center stitch line.

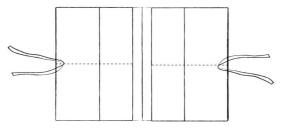

Sew ribbon to inside of bag 1" up from upper and lower edges

15 With the remaining length of olive variegated ribbon, tie knots along the length and loop the ribbon so there are three uneven loop drapes. Sew upper end of looped ribbon drape to front of bag. Sew knotted mum flower centered over looped ribbon drape.

Make looped ribbon drape with remaining piece of ribbon.

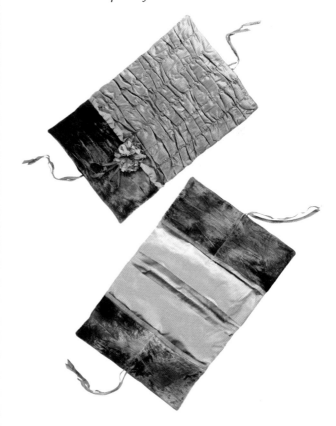

"Forget Me Nots"

"Make No Sound"

"Hear What No Ear Can Hear."

For project " A Poet's Garden"— Scan full color at 200%.

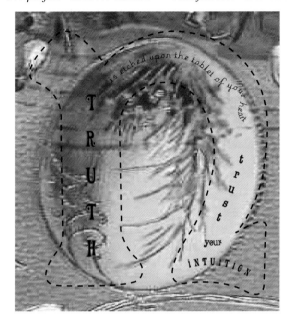

For project " See What No Eye Can See."

Scan full color at 100%
"Sky."

For project " Favorite Things"— Scan full color at 200%.

falling in love ❧ laughing out loud ❧ a chocolate milkshake ❧ taking a drive on a pretty road ❧ listening to your favorite song ❧ hearing the rain outside ❧ rereading your favorite book ❧ good conversation ❧ walking on the beach ❧ finding a twenty dollar bill in a coat pocket ❧ laughing at yourself ❧ having someone tell you you're beautiful ❧ being grateful for another beautiful day ❧ coming home ❧ giggling ❧ being pampered by your mom ❧ spending time with old friends ❧ sweet dreams ❧ your first kiss ❧ holding hands ❧ making chocolate chip cookies ❧ watching the sunrise ❧ hearing the ocean roar ❧ a road trip with friends ❧ falling in love ❧ laughing out loud ❧ a chocolate milkshake ❧ taking a drive on a pretty road ❧ listening to your favorite song ❧ hearing the rain outside ❧ rereading your favorite book ❧ good conversation ❧ walking on the beach ❧ finding a twenty dollar bill in a coat pocket ❧ laughing at yourself ❧ having someone tell you you're beautiful ❧ being grateful for another beautiful day ❧

"Favorite Things" Backdrop.

"Dress Sketch."

All images on these two pages are for project "Favorite Things" — Scan full color at 100%.

silks

"Silk Fabric Color Card."

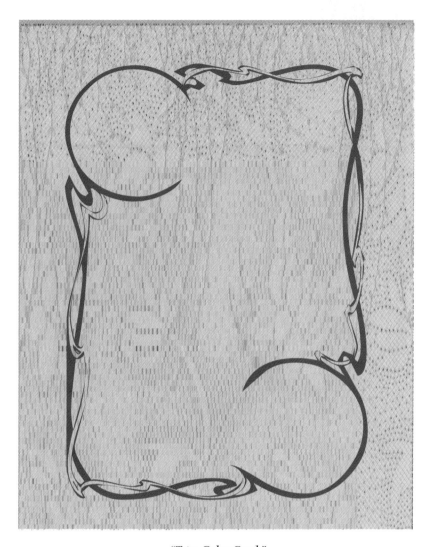

"Trim Color Card."

you
may
entertain
an
angel

"Angel Message."

Resources

Mary Jo Hiney Designs
PO Box 6205
Los Osos, CA 93412
www.maryjohineydesigns.com
Wholesale and Retail

Silk, Wool or Cotton Batting:
Hobbs Bonded Fibers
200 S. Commerce Drive
Waco, Texas 76710
800-433-3357
www.hobbsbondedfibers.com
Wholesale

Ribbonwork Kit shown on
"Wildly Charming"
From "Ribbonwork, The
Complete Guide," by Helen Gibb
Kit available directly from:
Helen Gibb Design Inc.
1002 Turnberry Circle
Louisville, CO
303-673-0949
www.helengibb.com
Retail

Bias cut silk ribbons:
Hanah Silk from Artemis
5155 Myrtle Avenue
Eureka, CA 95503
1-888-233-5187
www.artemisinc.com
Wholesale and Retail

Bias cut silk ribbons used on the
following projects:

"Creature Comforts," mauve
slippers: 1"-wide Stormy
Monday for bows

"Ignore the Rules", flower
bouquet: 1"-wide Stormy
Monday and Hot Flash

"Spread Your Wings" butterfly
pillows: 2½" and 1½"-wide
Wild Rose for draped ruffles

"Natural Beauties": Abalone
Silk Velvet hot quarter. 2½"-
wide Monet bias cut for ruffle.
7⁄16"-wide Passion Flower, Bali
Hai, Fresh Celery for knotted
mum. 7⁄16"-wide Green Tea
for ties.

Seed bead assortments
(Bead Soup and Bead Gravy):
Hofmann Originals
Rocklin, CA
916-624-1962
hofmannoriginals@prodigy.net
Wholesale and Retail

Vintage images printed
on cotton:
Home Arts
2620 East Windrim Court
Elk Grove, CA 95758
888-639-8570
www.ezhomearts.com
homearts@comcast.net
Retail

Color Hue Instant set
fabric dyes:
Maggie Backman
Things Japanese
9805 NE 116 St, PMB 7160
Kirkland, WA 98034-4248
425-821-2287
www.silkthing.com
Also available are silk machine
sewing threads
Retail

Journaling and stamping
type of supplies:
Studios Blackbird
1036.5 Chorro Street
San Luis Obispo, CA 93401
805-541-5198
orders@studiosblackbird.com
www.studiosblackbird.com
Retail and limited Wholesale

"Favorite Things": Dress Form
rubber stamp # 6111-G3.
Angel wings rubber stamp
#8772

Specialty Buttons
Susan Clarke Originals
2922 Quartz Hill Road
Redding, CA 96003
530-246-8880
www.susanclarkeoriginals.com
Wholesale and Retail

Publications
Krause Publications
700 E. State St.
Iola, WI 54990
800-258-0929
www.krausebooks.com

INFORMATION

"Silk Fabric Care: Handwashing Silks"
www.srfabrics.com

"Silk Fabrics and Terms"
www.wintersilks.com

"Glossary of Terms Related to Silk"
www.silkery.com

"Learn About Silk: A Buyer's
Guide to Silk Care, Sheets and
Bedding."
www.supercomfort.com

"India Crafts – Mirroring India in its
Crafts"
www.india-crafts.com

About the Author

Mary Jo's love for sewing and fabric is a gift from her mother and it was Mary Jo's sister who introduced her to the world of quilts. Owner of Mary Jo Hiney Designs and creator of Silk Adaptation, Mary Jo has been in the sewing, quilting and crafting industries since 1993 when the opportunity to design projects for book and magazine publishers lead to the authoring of numerous titles. Before that, Mary Jo was the owner of Something Special, Made By Hand, a manufacturer of handmade gifts and decorative accessories sold to the gift market. Mary Jo has a degree from the Fashion Institute of Design and Merchandising, having received the noteworthy Peacock Award upon graduation. Mary Jo has a sincere love for sewing and believes in the positive power of creativity. A favorite phrase, "for such a time as this," is spoken about and found in the book of Esther. Mary Jo is encouraged by these hopeful words that all of us can be what we are meant to be.

Learn to Take Your Sewing to New Levels

Thread Painting
Simple Techniques to Add Texture and Dimension
by Leni Levenson Wiener

Use your sewing machine, computer and creativity to design stunning custom fabric art using thread painting – one of today's most popular mediums. Discover hand-stitched artwork for totes, pillows, artwork for the home, and much more.

Softcover • 8¼ x 10⅞ • 128 pages
200+ color photos
Item# Z0379 • $24.99

Sew Any Fabric
A Quick Reference to Fabrics from A to Z
by Claire B. Shaeffer, with a foreward by Nancy Zieman

This handy, easy-to-use reference is filled with practical techniques that enable you to acquire confidence while you develop new skills stitching on various fabrics.

Softcover • 8¼ x 10⅞ • 160 pages
100 color photos • 50+ b&w illus.
Item# SAFB • $23.99

Stitch Spritz & Sew
Curved Piecing as Easy as 1-2-3
by Kathy Bowers

Pick up a quick and simple appliqué method for stitching on a curve, curved piecing that is. Create mirror image frames, and arcs all while learning how to add new design elements to basic quilting.

Softcover • 8¼ x 10⅞ • 128 pages
60 color photos
Item# Z1311 • $22.99

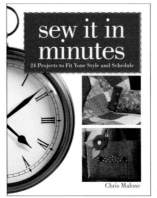

Sew It In Minutes
24 Projects to Fit Your Style and Schedule
by Chris Malone

Discover how to create each of the 24 projects in this book in 60, 90, 120, 240 minutes or less. Projects include ornaments, photo frames, an appliquéd bib and more.

Softcover • 8¼ x 10⅞ • 128 pages
175 color photos and illus.
Item# Z0133 • $22.99

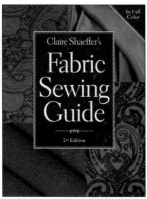

Claire Shaeffer's Fabric Sewing Guide
2nd Edition
by Claire Shaeffer

This full-color edition of the ultimate one-stop sewing resource is great for new and savvy sewers alike, with easy-to-read charts for needle sizes, and thread and stabilizer types.

Softcover • 8¼ x 10⅞ • 504 pages
75 b&w illus. • 225 color photos
Item# Z0933 • $39.99